RELEASE & CONTROL FOR IT SERVICE MANAGEMENT BASED ON ITIL®

D1807613

About the ITSM Library

The publications in the ITSM Library cover best practice in IT Management and are published on behalf of itSMF Netherlands (itSMF-NL).

The IT Service Management Forum (itSMF) is the association for IT service organizations, and for customers of IT services. itSMF's goal is to promote innovation and support of IT management; suppliers and customers are equally represented within the itSMF. The Forum's main focus is exchange of peer knowledge and experience. Our authors are global experts.

The following publications are, or soon will be, available.

Introduction, Foundations and Practitioners books
- Foundations of IT Service Management based on ITIL® / IT Service Management, an introduction - based on ITIL® (Arabic, Danish, German, English, French, Italian, Japanese, Chinese, Korean, Dutch, Portuguese, Russian, and Spanish)
- IT Services Procurement, an introduction based on ISPL (Dutch)
- Project management based on PRINCE2® (Dutch, English, German)
- Practitioner Release & Control for IT Service Management, based on ITIL® (English)

IT Service Management - best practices
- IT Service Management - best practices, part 1 (Dutch)
- IT Service Management - best practices, part 2 (Dutch)
- IT Service Management - best practices, part 3 (Dutch)

Topics & Management instruments
- Metrics for IT Service Management (English)
- Six Sigma for IT Management (English)
- The Request for Proposal (RfP) for IT Outsourcing (Dutch)
- Service Agreements (English)
- Frameworks for IT Management (English)

Pocket guides
- ISO/IEC 20000 - a pocket guide (English, German, Italian, Spanish, formerly BS 15000 - a pocket guide)
- IT Services Procurement based on ISPL - a pocket guide (English)
- IT Governance based on CobiT - a pocket guide (English, German)
- IT Service CMM - a pocket guide (English)
- IT Service Management - a summary based on ITIL® (Dutch)
- IT Service Management from hell! (English)

For any further enquiries about ITSM Library, please visit www.itsmfbooks.nl, http://en.itsmportal.net/en/node/14063 or www.vanharen.net.

Release & Control for IT Service Management
based on ITIL®

A PRACTITIONER GUIDE

Configuration Management,

Release Management &

Change Management

Colofon

Title:	Release & Control for IT Service Management based on ITIL®- a Practitioner Guide
Editors:	Jan van Bon (Chief Editor, itSMF-NL) Annelies van der Veen (Editor, Inform-IT)
Edition:	First edition, first impression, Januari 2007
ISBN (10):	90 8753 022 6
ISBN (13):	978 90 8753 022 8
Publisher:	Van Haren Publishing (info@vanharen.net)
Design & layout:	CO2 Premedia bv, Amersfoort – NL
Printer:	Wilco, Amersfoort - NL

Foreword

Professionals who use ITIL are often blamed for approaching things much too theoretical. To them, theory has become a rule instead of a guideline. They forget taking into account all specific factors that make an organization unique.

The authors of this book perfectly understood this: processes are not considered as independent entities, but as a logical and coherent clustering of related processes. And this is the very lesson we learned from over 10 years of intensive ITSM practice. It is the only road to successful service management.

The new Practitioner Cluster series approaches the ITSM processes in a logical way. In doing so, processes will be applied much easier. The book that lies before you is the first book in this series.

Any outsider will perceive the title of this book as rather puzzling. Putting Release and Control into one book seems like a contradiction. Release (letting go) and control (getting a grip) are not compatible. Nevertheless, this book discusses processes that are a huge challenge to every member of itSMF.
These days you just need to have a grip on IT service quality, but at the same time the environment keeps getting more complex and dynamic. In its turn, this requires more grip. Here a vicious circle emerges that makes the hairs of many IT professional turn grey.
This book will be of great help to anyone who recognizes this challenge.

To all students and professionals who use this book for exam preparation or for process improvement in their organization, I wish them: Relief and Control.

Arjen Droog
CEO ITSMF NL

Acknowledgements

itSMF Netherlands likes to thank the team of experts that have been involved in the development of this publication. We wish to thank all team members for generously sharing their knowledge, best practice and valuable time to deliver the contents for this first standardized Guide for the new Practitioner clusters. We owe them – and their companies - special thanks for sharing templates and best practice. This practical material makes the book into a valuable reference guide for all Release & Control professionals.

The book project was originally initiated by Lex Hendriks, portfolio manager of EXIN and was produced under guidance of Jan van Bon, chief editor of itSMF-NL.

The project team was composed of the major 'players' in the market: either the biggest training vendors in the Practitioner market, and, or the people that were involved in developing the clusters. This team was set up to represent the global market, to decide about the content of the common Practitioner cluster Guides, and to contribute to the development of these Practitioner Guides.

The draft TOC was developed by Hans van den Bent (Getronics PinkRoccade, NL), Jörn Oldag (Infora, Germany) and Pierre Bernard (Pink Elephant Inc., US/Canada). The project team discussed the ideal contents and subject matter of the book and after peer review reached a final agreement.

We wish to thank all team members for contributing to this book and participating in the thorough review process itSMF-NL applies to all its ITSM Library publications.

Co-authors

Hans van den Bent is Senior Training Consultant with Getronics PinkRoccade (Netherlands). Hans is an internationally experienced IT-Management trainer (ITIL, MOF and the ASP Industry) and holds the Management Certificate in IT Service Management, the Practitioner Certificate in Release and Control, ITIL Service Management training accreditations (as first tutor) with both the EXIN and ISEB examination institutes, and a master trainer accreditation for the Microsoft Operations Framework (MOF). Hans has co-authored and reviewed several books in the field of IT Service Management, such as: OGC Service Support, OGC the Business perspective, MOF pocket guide.

Pierre Bernard is the Manager of Education Services for Pink Elephant (Canada) responsible for a team of 15 trainers as well all ownership of all education products. With over 22 years of IT experience, the last seven with Pink Elephant, Pierre is dedicated to the improvement and growth of IT professionals and organizations. Pierre is a frequent contributor of exam questions for EXIN for all levels of ITIL® certifications. Pierre holds a Bachelor of Computer Sciences from Bishops University (Lennoxville, Québec) as well as the Manager Certificate in IT Service Management.

Michael Busch is a managing director of it SolutionCrew GmbH (Switzerland). Also, he is IT Service Management Consultant with main activities in Service Level Management, Change-, Configuration- and Release management in projects of medium to international coöperations. Michael is working for EXIN since 2001, in various roles and is enrolled in various itSMF activities. He is a Certified Service manager since 1999 and working in the field of service management since 1995. Also, he is a certified Internal auditor and Consultant for ISO 20 000.

Marcus Giese of TÜV Informatik und Consulting Services GmbH (Germany).

Lex Hendriks Lex is a Portfolio Manager for EXIN (Netherlands) and manages the EXIN portfolio of certification and associated services, including the I-Tracks program, certification for ITIL, project management, procurement management and service quality management (ISO20000). He contributed to the development and management of the ITIL certification program, in cooperation with ISEB and was involved in the update of the ITIL books as a member of the ITIL Advisory Group. Lex was co-founder and first chair of itSMF-NL. He is a member of the editorial board of the itSMF series IT Service Management best practices and contributed to several ITSM Library publications as reviewer or coauthor.

Georges Kemmerling is a Senior Consultant with Quint Wellington Redwood in Europe. He has been training and consulting on the subject for the past 10 years. His field of expertise covers most of the IT 'Best Practices' and he specialises in Management of Change.

Glenn LeClair is a Senior ITIL Consultant with HP (Canada). Glenn is a Certified Management Consultant and ITIL Service Manager and a member of the Institute of Service Management. Glenn is a former ITSM Canada Bookstore Manager and Humber College Instructor.

Moira Stepchuk is an independent consultant working with Fox IT USA and Pultorak & Associates. She has over 10 years of experience in Service Management consulting and training. She holds the Management Certificate in IT Service Management and is an accredited first tutor for ITIL Service Management training. She has specialized in guiding organizations on the practical application of ITIL and MOF and in the development of ITIL and MOF service offerings. Moira is a key contributor to ITIL courseware and MOF content and is a repeat presenter at the itSMF conferences. She is graduate of Villanova University in both Chemical Engineering and Masters of Business Administration.

Jose Tamo of QualiTI7 (Canada) is a Senior ITIL Consultant. During his career, he has worked in many sectors in Montreal, Canada, US and France in areas such as technical and application architecture, requirement analysis, team leadership, training, system integration and consulting for small and large enterprises as a ITIL consultant for which he has a Master certification. His expertise means he is invited to speak at conferences and facilitate training sessions at all ITIL levels.

Additional reviewers & co-authors
Besides the peer review of the authors, some team members have been of great value to the improvement of the book by thoroughly reviewing various drafts. We owe them special thanks

for generously offering extra time to write sections that were still missing and for their valuable advice during the last editorial phase.

Frederik van Eeden started his career in 1982 in system development and slowly got acquainted with maintenance and control of Information Systems. Since ITIL was introduced to him in 1992 (by Hans van den Bent), Frederik never let go of ITIL. He worked as a Change Manager, Service Desk Manager, IT Manager, and is now a passionate trainer for ISES International, teaching ITIL, System Development, Functional Control and more. Frederik is a Service Manager and co-author of a Database design book.

Adrian Leach worked for Parity, Putteridge Consultancy, during the starting phase of this project. Now he is a director of ITILPlus, that develops high quality and accredited (where appropriate) training and guidance materials that help organizations achieve business and IT alignment. Adrian provides advice and other help to organizations on a world-wide basis. He specializes in IS Lifecycle Management, including IS Strategy, Programme, Governance, Application, Service, ICT Infrastructure, Procurement, Contract, Transition, Quality, Change and Benefits Management. Adrian is actively involved with accreditation and examination panels.

Jörn Oldag is a senior consultant for IT Service Management with INFORA GmbH, Germany. His recent activities were focused on supporting IT service providers throughout Germany, especially in the public sector, with various coaching and training methods. Additional to his ITIL qualifications he works as a Prince 2 trainer and an ISO 20000 advisor.

Jean-Claude Baudry is an independent consultant in Service Management and is co-founder of the QualiTI7 network of independent workers. He is highly skilled in implementing IT service management (ITSM) processes based on globally recognized standards (ITIL framework). His experience with IT support environments and service desks as well as integration of change, release and configuration management enables him to accurately identify needs and market trends in ITSM. He is an active member of the itSMF community and also frequently participates to Service Management conference as speaker and participates in different redaction teams on the subject.

Contents

1 Introduction

1.1 Learn to practice

This book on IT Service Management Practitioner Release & Control aims to help the reader to use Best Practices in their role in the fields of Change Management, Release Management and Configuration Management.

The guidance provided in this book is based on version 2 of ITIL®, the Best Practice Library in IT Service Management (ITSM). The benefits of this publication are dual: it aims at both practitioners and students. It contains hands-on advice, not found in the ITIL books, from experienced practitioners from all over the world, but the book is also a valuable study aid for those preparing for the Practitioner Certificate in IT Service Management Release and Control.

Right from the start the originator of the ITIL concept recognized the need for a well-established training program and the recognition of professionals in the field through certification. In these training programs considerable attention is paid to the actual practice of IT Service Management, and their contents tends to reflect the most up-to-date view of what is the 'core' message, i.e. the 'philosophy' of the ITIL books. The internationally recognized certification is of key importance for all staff involved in IT Service Management.

If you, as an IT professional, regularly update your knowledge, for example in the field of IT Service Management, then your value as a professional, colleague and employee will naturally increase. An internationally recognized certificate is particularly valuable as it qualifies you for jobs requiring that particular knowledge and it may offer you the opportunity to launch a more fulfilling career.

Apart from your own personal satisfaction to remain competitive, it also brings professional recognition from both the industry and your peers.

The IT Service Management Practitioner Certificate is aimed at professionals involved in the day-to-day activities of managing IT Service Management processes. To specify the requirements for the Practitioner Certificate the key tasks of the Practitioner have been defined as:

- **Managing** - e.g. initiating and planning activities and reporting on the effectiveness and efficiency of the activities in the processes;
- **Organizing** - e.g. coordinating and monitoring activities, exchanging information, and maintaining procedures;
- **Optimizing** - e.g. monitoring, auditing and optimizing processes and proposing improvements.

The names of these key tasks may vary between organizations and geographical areas. In one environment 'managing' will be known as 'planning', while elsewhere 'organizing' may be referred to as 'managing'.

The best preparation for a role as Practitioner is a combination of training and experience. The accredited ITSM Practitioner training courses offer a mix of guidance based on best practice, as documented in the ITIL books, and training in the application of this guidance in practice. A book supporting such training can only be a workbook.

The concept of learn to practice also perfectly fits the philosophy behind the Practitioner Certificate in IT Service Management. The Practitioner Certificate is part of the IT Service Management Certification program.

1.2   The Diamond of IT Service Management Certification

The 'Diamond of IT Service Management Certification' takes its name from the ITIL diamond-shaped overview of the core of ITIL, displaying the subjects in IT Service Management in four (diamond shaped) quadrants:

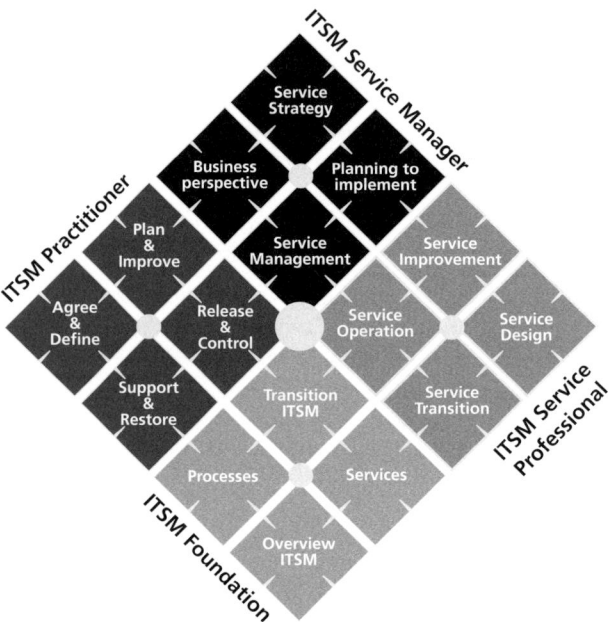

Figure 1.1   The Diamond of IT Service Management Certification

Each of the quadrants corresponds to a certain level of certification:
• **Foundation** (green) - The Foundation Certificate in IT Service Management recognizes a foundation level of knowledge in IT Service Management. It aims at all people who wish to become familiar with the best practices in IT Service Management, as defined in the IT Infrastructure Library (ITIL) guidelines. In particular, it enables people to understand the terminology used within the ITIL approach.
• **Practitioner** (blue) - The Practitioner Certificates in IT Service Management demonstrate the proficiency of those taking part in managing and optimizing specific processes within the IT Service Management discipline, and performing the activities that belong to those processes.
• **Service Professional** (yellow) - The Service Professional Certificate in IT Service Management acknowledges the professional skills to apply best practices in IT Service Management to optimize the IT Services and the IT Service Management processes.

• **IT Service Manager** (red) - The Manager's Certificate in IT Service Management indicates capability to manage ITIL-based solutions across the breadth of the Service Management subjects.

The current ITSM certification program consists of three of the four types of certificates mentioned above. The certification for the yellow quadrant, Service Professional , is under development.

The Practitioner quadrant consists of four certificates. The training topics for these certificates can be found in the overview, and are based on the life cycle of an IT service.

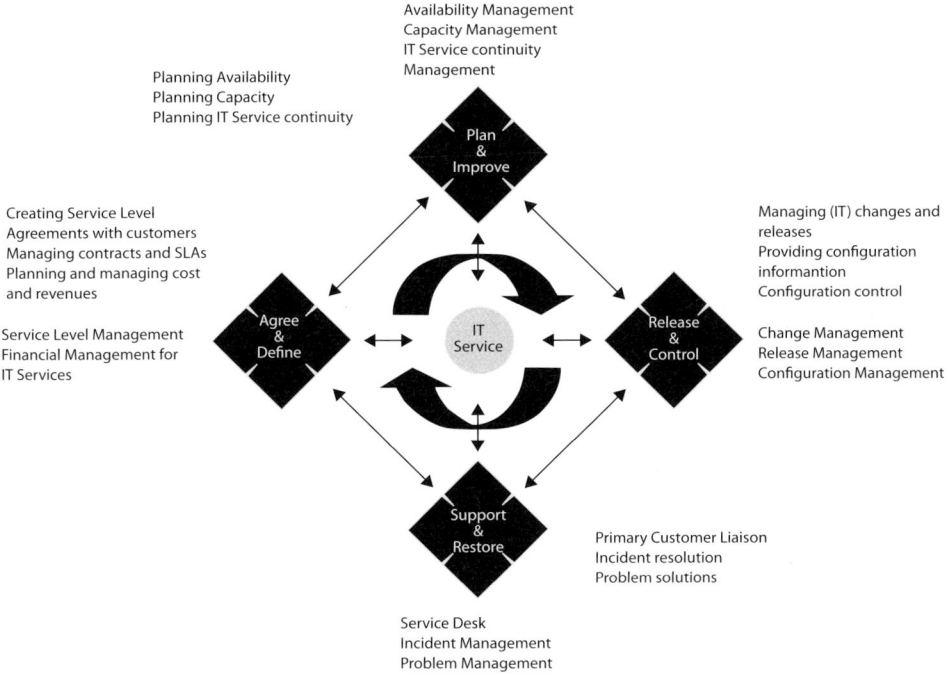

Figure 1.2   Overview of Practitioner Clusters

1.3   Practitioner Certificate in IT Service Management Release and Control

The Practitioner Certificate in IT Service Management Release and Control (IPRC) is aimed at professionals who will participate in managing and optimizing the operations of the Release & Control processes in an IT Service Organization which has already implemented these processes based on the ITIL guidance.
The target group consists of operational staff and managers wishing to extend their skills in planning, monitoring, reporting and optimizing, related to Change, Release and Configuration Management. They should have obtained basic knowledge of IT Service Management as indicated by their ITSM Foundation Certificate. Possession of the ITSM Foundation Certificate

is mandatory for those who wish to gain the Practitioners certificate and is a pre-requisite for taking the relevant examinations.

The Practitioner Release & Control certificate is of special interest for IT staff with some experience in one or more of the processes Configuration Management, Change Management or Release Management. It is also of interest to those who want to become involved in managing these processes within their organization.

Practitioners may be process managers, but they are also member of a team responsible for one or several processes - or a set of activities in these processes.

In practice, process manager tasks are often delegated, either because of the complexity of the organization, outsourcing or outtasking, or the existence of special groups of customers or specialized groups of IT staff who need to be involved in IT Service Management activities. The Practitioner will not necessarily have formal supervising powers over colleagues, but in general will play a directing role in a substantial part of the process.

Generally it will not be part of the role of the Practitioner to determine the organizations policy, for example the pricing policy for IT Services. Usually it would not fit into the Practitioner's role to implement a process from scratch. On the other hand, staff involved in the execution of activities in a process who do not have any responsibility in planning, monitoring or optimizing the process would not be regarded as an IT Service Management Practitioner. For example, Service Desk staff, who are mainly involved in registering calls and routing them to the appropriate specialist groups, according to existing procedures, would not be regarded as Practitioners. Neither would System Administrators involved in the installation of new hardware be regarded as Change Management Practitioners unless they also had some responsibility in managing and organizing the change process.

Examples of roles in the field of the Practitioner in IT Service Management Release & Control:
• Process manager (for the Change, Configuration or Release Management process)
• Staff of the centralized function Change, Release and Configuration Management
• Change Controller / Change Coordinator
• Configuration Controller / Configuration Management Coordinator
• Release Controller / Release Management Coordinator

Note that the names of the roles mentioned will vary from company to company.

The key tasks for the Practitioner IT Service Management Release & Control are:
• **managing** the Release & Control processes - e.g. initiating and planning activities and reporting on the effectiveness and efficiency of the activities in the processes;
• **organizing** the Release & Control processes - e.g. coordinating and monitoring activities, exchanging information, and maintaining procedures;
• **optimizing** the Release & Control processes - e.g. monitoring, auditing and optimizing processes and proposing improvements.

The chapters in this book are arranged on the three basic management principles of IT Service Management: Manage, Organize and Optimize.

2   ITIL Overview

2.1   IT Service Management

ITIL was developed in recognition of the fact that organizations are becoming increasingly dependent on IT to fulfill their corporate objectives. This increasing dependence has resulted in a growing need for IT services which correspond to the objectives of the business, and which meet the requirements and expectations of the customer.

In the 1980s a major shift occurred in the business world. With the rise of the Personal Computer, networking and client/server technologies, businesses became more capable of quickly developing new products and services. Production processes became more flexible, enabling tailoring according to demand. At the same time marketing started switching from praising a product for its technical features to praising products for their complementary services. In those years IT changed its position from a purely administrative function to a business driving function. The area where this was most noticeable was that of financial services.

In the overall life cycle of IT products, the operations phase amounts to about 70 to 80 per cent of the overall time and cost; the rest is spent on product development (or procurement). Thus, effective and efficient IT Service Management processes are essential to the success of IT. This applies to any type of organization, large or small, public or private, with centralized or decentralized IT services, and internal or outsourced IT services. In all cases, the service has to be reliable, consistent, of a high quality, and of acceptable cost.

In the diagram the customer discusses and agrees with the Development team as to the functional requirements of new (versions of) software. These functional requirements are based on business needs. The customer also discusses and agrees with representatives of Operations (the Service Level Manager) about support hours, about the 'non-functional requirements' such as support, about performance and uptime of the application. Finally Development and Operations need to exchange information about platforms and other technical requirements of the application. If the three types of specifications are not managed properly, the new application will not satisfy the customer.

ITIL concerns itself mainly with the operational part of the IT Infrastructure. ITIL addresses the provision and support of IT services tailored to the needs of the organization. It liaises with the customer and with (external) development organizations in order to guarantee the operational quality of IT services. In general an IT service can be described as: 'making available IT functionality to the customer'.

By using a process approach, ITIL describes what must be included in IT Service Management to provide IT services to the required quality. The structure and allocation of tasks and responsibilities between functions and departments depends on the type of organization, and these structures vary widely among IT departments and often change.

The description of the process structure provides a common point of reference that changes less rapidly. This structure can help maintain the quality of IT services during and after reorganizations and also among suppliers and partners as they change. The main body of knowledge of ITIL lies in the 10 processes of Delivery and Support. They are the core of ITIL and are often referred to as the processes of IT Service Management.

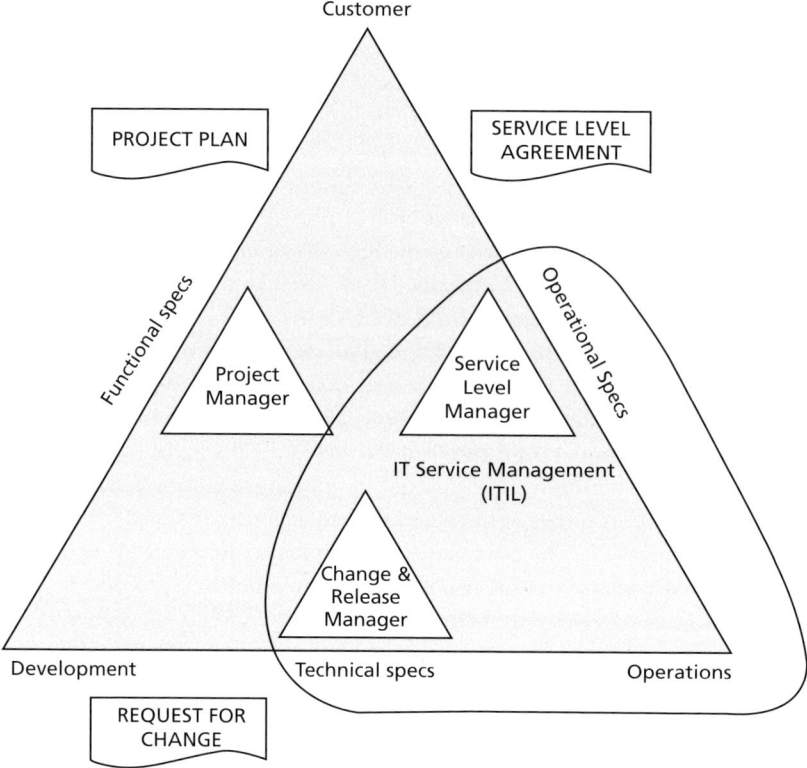

Figure 2.1   IT life cycle

2.2   ITIL Infrastructure

An infrastructure is needed to develop a 'best practice' in the market. The ITIL Infrastructure contains a standards organization that guards the materials (OGC), a user organization that organizes seminars and congresses (itSMF), a certification authority that allows professionals to get certifications at different levels (EXIN and ISEB), and commercial suppliers such as tool developers, book publishers and consultancy firms.

2.2.1   OGC (CCTA)

ITIL® was originally a CCTA product. CCTA was the Central Computer and Telecommunications Agency of the UK government. As of 1 April 2001, the CCTA was amalgamated with the OGC (Office of Government Commerce), which is now the new owner of ITIL. The objective of the OGC is to help its customers in the UK public sector update their procurement activities and improve their services by making the best possible use of IT and other instruments. 'OGC aims to modernize procurement in government, and deliver substantial value for money improvements.' The OGC promotes the use of 'best practices' in many areas (e.g. project management, procurement and IT Service Management). The OGC publishes several series (libraries) of books written by UK and international experts from a range of companies and organizations.

The OGC IT Infrastructure Library consists of a number of clear and thorough 'Codes of Practice' to provide efficient and effective IT services.

2.2.2 itSMF

The Information Technology Service Management Forum (itSMF), originally known as the Information Technology Infrastructure Management Forum (ITIMF), is the only internationally recognized and independent user group dedicated to IT Service Management. It is owned and operated solely by its membership. The itSMF is a major influence and contributor to Industry Best Practice and Standards worldwide.

The first chapter of itSMF was set up in the UK in 1991. The Dutch itSMF (itSMF The Netherlands) was the next chapter, set up in November 1993. There are now itSMF chapters in countries including South Africa, Belgium, Germany, Japan, Canada, the United States, and Australia, which cooperate in itSMF International.

itSMF chapters promote the exchange of information and experience which enables IT organizations to improve the services they provide. They organize seminars, conferences, special subject evenings, and other events about current IT Service Management subjects. They also publish newsletters and operate a website for information sharing. Task forces also contribute to the development of ITIL.

2.2.3 EXIN and ISEB

The Dutch 'EXamination Institute for INformation Science' (EXIN) and the UK 'Information Systems Examination Board' (ISEB) jointly developed a professional certification program for IT Service Management, based on ITIL. This was done in close cooperation with the OGC and itSMF. EXIN and ISEB are non-profit organizations that cooperate to offer a full range of ITSM qualifications at three levels:
- **Foundation Certificate** in IT Service Management
- **Practitioner Certificate** in IT Service Management
- **Manager's Certificate** in IT Service Management

The certification system is based on the requirements for effectively fulfilling the relevant role within an IT organization. To date, Foundation Certificates have been awarded to over 50,000 IT professionals in over 30 countries.

The Foundation Certificate is intended for all personnel who have to be aware of the major tasks in the IT organization, and the relationships between them. The Foundations examination covers the Service Desk function, and the processes for Incident Management, Problem Management, Change Management, Configuration Management, Release Management, Service Level Management, Availability Management, Capacity Management, IT Service Continuity Management, Financial Management for IT Services, and Security Management. After obtaining the Foundation Certificate, the Practitioner and Manager examinations can be undertaken. Practitioners are trained on a practical level how to perform specific IT Service Management processes or tasks for one process such as Service Level Management, or for processes that are grouped together like the IPRC which deals with Configuration Management, Release Management and Change Management. Managers are trained on a theoretical level how to control all the processes as listed under the Foundations certificate, how to advise about the structure and optimization of the processes, and how to implement them.

Today, ITIL represents much more than a series of useful books on IT Service Management. The framework of best practice in IT Service Management is an entire industry of organizations, tools, education and consulting services, related frameworks and publications. Since the 1990s, ITIL is not only considered to be the framework, but also the approach and philosophy shared by those using IT Service Management best practices in their work. A range of organizations cooperates internationally to promote ITIL as the de facto standard in IT Service Management. Although ITIL started its development as a 'best practice' it has been greatly been influenced by trends in the business market such as Total Quality Management, Business Process engineering and Value Chain management.

2.3   Overview of processes

The main body of ITIL consists of ten processes, also called the **ITIL core processes** or 'the processes of **IT Service Management**'. They are divided into two groups, the operational or support processes, and the tactical or delivery processes.

Below you will find a short synopsis of these 11 core processes:

Support processes:
1. **Incident Management** – to help users back to work. This process focuses on fire-fighting, not on root-cause analysis. It records all incidents, and registers, classifies and tracks them throughout their life cycle.
2. **Problem Management** – to find the root cause of re-occurring incidents and propose structural improvements to the infrastructure.
3. **Configuration Management** – to provide information on the IT infrastructure to support all kinds of decision making. The process keeps track of all IT service related assets during their life cycle and records versions, status and interdependencies.
4. **Change Management** – to absorb change without negatively impacting the business. The process records, coordinates and checks all change activity in the IT Infrastructure, with a special focus on impact and the availability of resources.
5. **Release Management** – to improve the reliability of operational software. The process sets up and monitors release policies, procedures and safe storage arrangements, needed to guard software and hardware masters, and organizes controlled roll-outs (and fall-backs).

Delivery processes:
1. **Service Level Management** – to manage customer expectations and supplier performance, by updating and documenting service requirements in agreements and by monitoring and reporting service delivery.
2. **Availability Management** – to agree and manage acceptable repair-time and resiliency for business (critical) systems, including external support contracts, at acceptable costs.
3. **Capacity Management** – to monitor and manage system performances and trends in resource usage, and to manage services for optimum resource usage.
4. **IT Services Continuity Management** – to prepare arrangements to restore service in the event of a disaster.
5. **Financial Management for IT Services** – to address matters of cost structuring, budgeting and charging for IT services.
6. **Security Management** - to provide the level of security necessary for the provision of the total service to the organisation.

Apart from these core processes, ITIL also describes a function: the **Service Desk**. This function combines activities from several of the listed processes.

All 11 processes and the Service Desk are covered in the scope of the ITSM Foundation exam.

2.4   Process goals and objectives

Each of these processes or functions is designed to support the goals and objectives of the services organization. The following chapters will go into detail on this. But before looking at goals and objectives, it is important to take a step back and to understand their relationships with an organization's vision and mission.

Organizations often summarize goals and objectives into a vision and/or a mission statement. It is important to properly define and comprehend the meaning of various management terms such as vision, mission, goals and objectives.

Vision and Mission

The vision of an organization can be described as 'an image of the future we seek to create'. Therefore, a vision statement will describe in graphic terms where the organizational goal-setters want to see the organization in the future.

The mission of an organization on the other hand can be defined as its 'purpose, reason for being'. A mission statement defines the purpose or broader goal for being in existence or in the business. It serves as a guide in times of uncertainty, vagueness. It is like guiding light. It has no time frame.

Some features of an effective vision statement:
• is clear and unambiguous
• paints a vivid, clear picture
• describes a bright future
• is memorable and engaging
• is aligned with organizational values and culture
• is S.M.A.R.T. (Specific, Measurable, Achievable, Realistic and Time-bound)

In order to become really effective, an organizational vision statement must be embedded into the organization's culture. Leaders at all levels of the organization have the responsibility of communicating the vision regularly, create narratives that illustrate the vision, act as role-models by embodying the vision, create short-term objectives compatible with the vision, and encourage others to craft their own personal vision compatible with the organization's overall vision.

Goals and objectives

Goals and objectives serve to eliminate the gap between current situation and desired state. Goals are defined as 'inexactly formulated aims that lack specificity' while objectives are defined as 'aims formulated exactly and quantitatively as to time-frames and magnitude of effect'. People often make goals and objectives synonymous. For the purpose of Continual Service Improvement, this is not the case.

When the goals and objectives are in place, they must be communicated to the appropriate people. It is not enough to simply send an email to these people explaining what the goals are; the goals must be communicated. There is a significant difference between providing information and communicating.

2.5   Organizational context

The line organization as we know it is a product of the industrial era. In it functional units, like customer service and network management, are grouped around specialisms. This enables the organization to make the most efficient use of its resources. In a factory, controlling costs and efficiency are all that counts. In this environment managers have a direct say in the distribution of work and they make operational decisions on a daily basis. Employees are monitored by their completion of pre-specified activities. Control in such an organization is centralized. A factory is not a customer friendly organization; the culture is usually an inward-looking culture, focused on running machines. Customers can only disturb such a process.

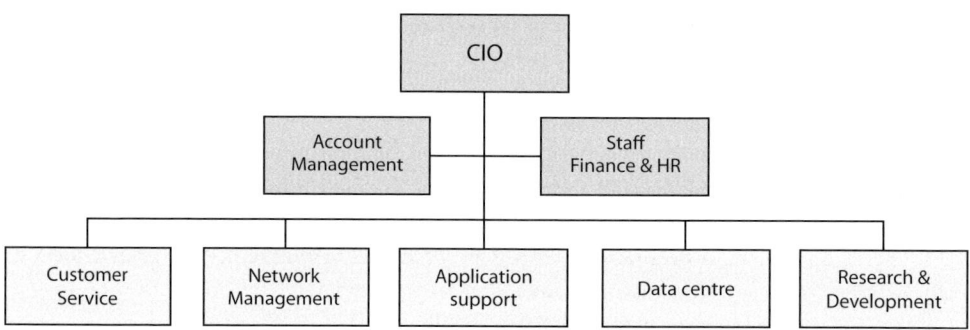

Figure 2.2   The IT department

In the 1980s the service industry expanded and that created the need for a different type of organization. Imagine the following scenario:

In order to apply for a mortgage at your local bank, you have to apply for a loan at the private credit department. As collateral you offer your real estate and a portfolio of securities which are managed by the investment department. The securities should, in 30 years, cover the loan. In case of unemployment or in case of your death you want to apply for some insurance from the insurance department. All these financial services should fit nicely together but you have absolutely no experience with these banking disciplines!

In come the generalists. They know enough about all the different disciplines to be able to integrate the different services. They also understand the wishes of the customer, thereby making it easier for them to identify and develop new services. That is why they will come up with new services all the time. This only works if the generalists can, to some extent, prioritize the workloads in the different specialist departments and initiate the development of new cross-departmental services and products. They need to have a mandate. In a factory environment, generalists usually don't fit in. Generalists are not managed by simply mapping the daily processes they perform, like specialists. They are best managed by being given targets and operating criteria: by agreeing the results that they must produce and by agreeing the limitations within which they can operate;

'we are a steak restaurant and we don't sell fish'. This is why generalists are usually put in a front-office where they are managed in a different way from the factory. In the front-office you will find account managers, Service Level Managers, Service Desk staff, a project and change request desk, etc. The front-office is not organized in functional departments but in customer teams or service teams containing an account manager, a service level manager, Service Desk personnel, etc.

The problem with ITIL: most IT organizations are still run like factories. This means that their primary process is: 'to keep the machines running'. They will do this at a reasonable cost and efficiency, as long as the customer doesn't make life difficult for them with special demands. A factory is a good option if you can standardize and simplify your IT services to a great extent. Management can give some people ITIL training, but they still run the organization like a factory and often aren't even aware of it.

If, however, the aim of the IT organization is 'to supply services to the customer', a front-office is needed with generalists who are sufficiently mandated to prioritize the activities in the factory. As a result the factory will operate less efficiently, but will provide better services to the customer. Line managers will find it hard to manage such a factory because they lose some grip on the efficiency of their department. Organizations who claim that they want to be a factory AND a service company risk creating an organization where priorities are unclear and decisions are hard to make.

2.6   Managing a service company

Factories have, what is traditionally called, a role culture (Harisson and Handy). A role culture is the result of optimizing a production process in a steady environment. It is geared towards efficiency and it is an inward looking culture that tries to describe the production process in minute steps. Employees in a role culture see themselves as a small part of the production machine. They do not feel responsible for the result - a happy customer -, because their part in the production has become so small that they feel they can't really influence it. If the service fails, it will be due to the complexity of the machine; 'I did the best I could with the input that I got'.

A service culture is a culture in which employees feel responsible for the results, as long as they feel that they are directly related to having a happy customer. They take initiatives and are sufficiently empowered to exercise their responsibility. Management empowers employees through clear policies which create the framework within which employees can act independently. Job profiles are based on result areas rather than on functional task descriptions.

A service company is similar to a well-run restaurant. It is less structured and everybody pulls his weight. When the waiter returns to the kitchen he brings some empty glasses, even if it isn't his role to clean the table. If he doesn't bring the empties, someone will reproach him for it. When implementing ITIL these two cultures will clash; 'how can I run a good kitchen if all these waiters keep telling me what to do …?'

3 Introduction Release & Control

3.1 Introduction

The rapid development of IT technology and the business market have had high impact on the level of change in the organization. Business needs to improve their services and reduce their costs and needs IT to support and to be part of the continuing business change process.

Managing the changes in IT and IT services and maintaining the control over the IT infrastructure is the common core mission of the Release & Control processes: Release Management, Change Management and Configuration Management. The goal of the Release & Control processes is to effectively and timely introduce those changes that are approved, with minimal disruption of the IT services.

The Change Management process takes care of the management of all changes, ensuring that they are properly assessed, approved, recorded, planned, implemented, reviewed and tracked in line with customer requirements.

In a managed IT environment disruption of IT Services by introducing, modifying or and retracting software or hardware is often minimized by deployment of such changes in releases, carefully composed sets of changes that are to be implemented together. Coordination of the releases is done by Release Management, addressing all technical and non-technical aspects of the changes in a release.

A controlled IT environment requires reliable and up-to-date information on the details of the IT infrastructure. This information should not only include details on specific components of the infrastructure, Configuration Items, but also show how these CIs exactly are related and mutually dependent on each other.

The Configuration Management process will have to produce the information on which the other IT Service Management processes rely. Hence, all changes will have to be recorded properly in the Configuration Management Database (CMDB).

The activities of the Release & Control processes are highly interdependent. For example, normally the scope of the Configuration Management Database (CMDB) will be identical to the scope of the Change Management process, and all changes in a release will be managed by Change Management.

It is best practice to form a single team responsible for these three processes. Such a Release & Control team will be a natural coordination point between the teams responsible for developing service solutions and the operations teams running the IT Services in production.

3.2 Manage, Organize, Optimize

The activities of the Release & Control processes are divided into three groups, according to the main activities of a Practitioner: Managing, Organizing and Optimizing (alternatively listed as: Planning, Managing and Optimizing).

3.2.1 Managing the Change, Release and Configuration Management processes

The way the Release & Control processes are managed will depend on many situational factors, including the complexity and culture of the organization, and the type of business of the customers of the IT services.

The actual Release & Control team may consist of one single person in a small IT department or involve a worldwide network of specialist groups in an international company.

Management of the Release & Control processes should preferably be based on a combined Management Plan for Release, Change and Configuration Management.
The main input to the Management Plan will be delivered from the process owner. They will define the conditions / restrictions under which the processes will have to operate. At the same time the Critical Success Factors (CSFs) are defined which need to be achieved to meet the required level of service from the business or client. Key Performance Indicators (KPIs)are set within the process to help improve the process continually to a higher quality level. The continual quality improvement needs to be monitored and reported on a regular basis to the process owner, in order to allow adequate intervention in case the Business Requirements or Service Requirements have changed.
The Release & Control processes are largely depending on the overall agreement with the customer, as these are set in the Release Policy. If the service provider has agreed to a specific release calendar, then even an urgent change may be subject to this calendar - or cannot be implemented without explicit agreement of the customer.

The Management Plans are the basic needs for the management of the processes and need approval of senior management. Reports for senior management on the effectiveness and efficiency of the Release & Control processes will also be based on the process management plans.
The key activitiesin each of the processes are described in next chapters of this book.

To be able to plan each of these activities:
• The objectives, scopes and activities should be described.
• Roles and responsibilities need to be assigned.
• Appropriate training for personnel will have to be defined.
• Policies should be defined related processes regarding Release &Control procedures.
• Standards and quality criteria need to be defined and applied.
• Requirements will have to be defined for tool selection.

Procedures should be established or amended for:
• initiation of RFCs
• handling urgent changes
• impact and resource assessment of RFCs
• scheduling issues related to RFCs
• building and testing of changes
• implementing changes
• post implementation reviews of changes
• planning releases

- designing, building and configuring releases
- release acceptance
- roll-out planning of releases
- communication, preparation and training regarding releases
- distribution and installation of releases
- configuration management planning
- configuration identification and CIs
- configuration control
- configuration status accounting
- configuration verification and audit

The Configuration Management Plan is the basic need for the definition of the configuration baselines, the Configuration Management Database (CMDB), the Definitive Software Library (DSL) and the Definitive Hardware Store (DHS).

Managing the Release & Control processes also includes designing and planning the exchange of information between the Release & Control processes and between these processes and the other Service Management processes, as well as ensuring that the business requirements and prerequisites are met.
This requires:
- a detailed description of the relationships between Change Management, Release Management and Configuration Management
- identification of the information to be delivered to other Service Management processes
- identification of the information that must come from other Service Management processes

To enable the exchange of information with other processes the practitioners in the Release & Control team need commitment from the practitioners in other processes. It is of utmost importance in such communication processes that the practitioners in Release & Control must be able to explain the benefits of the Release & Control processes and the benefits of a combined change, release and configuration plan.

Managing the Release & Control processes also requires initiating actions to ensure the key activities in the Release & Control processes meet the objectives set. In practice this means:
- defining metrics and reports that enable informed decision making
- identifying and managing key issues that may impact the effective operation of the Release & Control processes

Report on the effectiveness and efficiency of the activities

Like any other Service Management process, the Release & Control processes will have to report on the effectiveness and efficiency of the activities in the Release & Control processes, with an agreed frequency.
But what do you report on? In order to demonstrate the effectiveness and efficiency of a process, the Critical Success Factors Factors (CSFs) and Key Performance Indicators (KPIs) must be identified. It is recommended that no more than two to three CSFs be considered at any given time, and that no more than two to three KPIs per CSF are measured. This represents between four to nine KPIs for one process. Multiply this by the number of processes and you may end up

with nearly one hundred KPIs. There are ten processes in Service Support and Service Delivery, plus Security Management plus the Service Desk.

Reporting on effectiveness means reporting on *doing the right thing*, such as compliance to the process, while reporting on efficiency means reporting on *doing things right*, such as reducing the time it takes to do something.
Typically the reports required will include:
• reports based on the process deliverables and explaining what reports are possible
• general reports related to changes, releases and configurations for business management, IT management and the managers of the Support processes, Service Level Management and Availability Management process
• reports concerning risks, impact, urgency, priority, bottlenecks, problems, evaluation and review and quality standards

To be able to draw up such reports:
• the type and format of reports required within the organization must be identified
• the Key Performance Indicators (KPIs) for the Release & Control processes must be monitored

3.2.2 Organizing the Change, Release and Configuration Management processes
The interaction between the various IT Service Management processes is very important in order to deliver a high quality IT Service. Therefore it is vital that the Change, Release and Configuration Management processes:
• deliver appropriate information to other Service Management processes, including Application and Infrastructure Management
• get appropriate information from other Service Management processes, including Application and Infrastructure Management

In order to ensure continuous support for the Change, Release and Configuration Management processes it is necessary to communicate the purpose and benefits of Change Management, Release Management and Configuration Management within the organization.

Delivering Information
The Change, Release and Configuration Management needs to deliver information to all IT Service Management processes and the Service Desk, concerning:
• the configuration, infrastructure and all other service relevant aspects
• the planned changes and releases
• the Forward Schedule of Changes and Release Calendar
• the Projected Service Availability

At the same time Configuration Management will deliver information to all interested external parties within the company / organization or other business processes.

The communication / information between all interested parties will be done by holding regular meetings in which all Release Management matters are discussed, such as training and communication plans for new releases.

Ongoing Management of the Release & Control Processes

The day-to-day management of the Release & Control Processes demand the following activities to be carried out:

- translate customer needs and requirements into input for the Release & Control Processes
- translate Release & Control procedures into daily work activities
- analyze the current configuration
- plan and implement an initial capture of data for the Configuration Management Database (CMDB)
- manage and maintain the CMDB to ensure that it is consistent and up-to-date
- organize CMDB back-ups, archives and housekeeping
- implement procedures for the registration of new CIs and removal of written-off CIs
- manage the Definitive Software Library (DSL) and the Definitive Hardware Store (DHS)
- manage and use Change, Release and Configuration Management tools
- make proposals for naming conventions for configuration items (CIs)
- identify attributes and relationships for configuration items (CIs)
- create procedures for license management
- maintain change models
- maintain impact and priority coding systems
- maintain the classification of RFCs
- maintain procedures for convening and running Change Advisory Board (CAB) meetings
- establish release identification
- make sufficient resources and time available for building, testing and implementing releases
- produce roll-out and release plans for each release
- ensuring business, Application Management and other key impacted areas remain aware of release issues.

Defining Procedures and regulations

Whenever a change to the infrastructure is carried out it is necessary to define the baseline from which the change starts and to which one has to return, in case the change cannot be successfully implemented.

It is necessary that the Release & Control processes have procedures in place that will allow you:

- to identify the configuration baselines
- to properly execute configuration status accounting.

Release Management

Every update that is released within the organization needs to be well defined and appropriately managed when introduced into the infrastructure. All releases need to be carried out taking the needs of the IT Service customers and business into account.

The following processes need to be adopted when releasing into the live IT infrastructure environment:
- all license information is recorded against software CI records and this is checked during the software distribution process;
- ensure that all CIs within a release are traceable, secure and that only correct, authorized and tested versions are installed;
- check that the exact content and roll-out of releases is agreed with Change Management;
- produce operating and support documentation for each release;
- plan and design the build and test environment;
- establish release and distribution procedures for hardware and software; and
- design and build the releases.

Whenever a change is carried out in the IT Infrastructure an appropriate back-out plan needs to be defined. The complexity of such a plan will depend on the change carried out.

A change that alters a vast number of different CIs will require a more sophisticated back-out plan than a change that alters a single CI. The single CI may have no impact on the business if it cannot be changed successfully within the defined time, but a vast number of CIs are bound to have significant effect, if something goes wrong.

A back-out plan will consist of:
- the procedure description of how to back-out;
- test plans on when to initiate the back-out plan;
- test plans on when the back-out will be considered successful.

In any case, it is necessary to define for each release:
- acceptance criteria and test results;
- training plans for staff involved.

All changes taking place in the IT Infrastructure need to be documented and recorded in the CMDB. It is therefore necessary to define procedures and operational rules and regulations that will:
- ensure the CMDB is updated to reflect new or modified components within a release;
- describe how to distribute and implement the release unit;
- ensure that master copies of all software in a release are secured in the DSL, and that the CMDB is updated;
- describe how to manage the DHS; and
- state how to manage the documentation regarding releases.

Change Management
All changes taking place within the IT infrastructure must, at all times, be managed and controlled, whether these are standard changes within the initial change schedule or urgent changes, caused by incidents.

The following tasks have to be performed to ensure that a change is managed and handled in a proper way:
- assess the business, technical and financial impact of changes;
- plan and prioritize changes centrally or by common agreement;
- assist the Change Manager in preparing a CAB meeting;
- coordinate approval (authorizing), scheduling and implementation of changes;
- allocate the necessary resources for planned changes;
- issue a schedule of approved changes and a Forward Schedule of Changes (FSC);
- monitor change progress adequately;
- monitor the creation and testing of back-out plans;
- monitor the review of changes; and
- close the change record, based on a successful review.

Configuration Management
In order to be able to deliver accurate information to all interested internal and external parties Configuration Management needs to ensure that:
- all configuration items are uniquely identified;
- configuration control is in place and all changes to Configurations Items are recorded and documented in the CMDB;
- the information stored in the CMBF is regularly verified; and
- configuration audits are carried out regularly in order to ensure that the information corresponds with the reality.

Configuration Management will support the Change and Release Management Process by:
- generating and storing configuration baselines whenever a change is taking place, in order to be able to revert to this baseline if necessary; and
- generating a status account for each CI involved in a change and in subsequent releases.

The basis of the Configuration Management Process is the Configuration Management Database (CMDB). This database is the central source of all information concerning the Configuration Items, including their interrelationship and mutual dependency.

3.2.3 Optimizing the Change, Release and Configuration Management processes
The continual monitoring and review of the release and control procedures, systems and tools is necessary to ensure that the desired process outputs are generated. Therefore, it is necessary to:
- analyze the output of the process regarding the Key Performance Indicators (KPIs); and
- define new or improved reports, documents, procedures, instructions or tools.

Whenever an audit or monitoring activity reveals that the process or the output of the process does not conform to the goals and regulations defined, it is necessary to propose and implement appropriate changes to the release and control processes. These changes should be based on results of monitoring and/or reviews.

An integral task that the Change, Release and Configuration Management process needs to perform is the planning of audits, to ensure adherence to the defined processes. Only when these audits are carried out regularly, the process performance, and thereby the service quality, will be as designed. Overall, the following three tasks need to be planned and conducted:

* implement procedures and work instructions to help coordinate verification and audits of CIs;
* audit the real situation against the CMDB; and
* establish review meetings.

Another way to optimize the performance of the processes is standardization.
All of these optimization examples can be handled in the perspective of a continual PDCA cycle, according to Deming (Plan, Do, Check, Act).

3.3   Relationships with other processes

Incident Management
Incident Management uses information from Configuration Management to determine the CIs involved in an incident, relate incidents to problems or known errors with a workaround, and identify which services are impacted and which SLAs or contracts affected.
Change Management puts through changes requested by Incident Management to take away the effect of incidents. Changes may also introduce incidents and Incident Management should be informed on the implementation of changes, to quickly identify and remedy any related incidents.

Problem Management
Problem Management relies on the information from Configuration Management to link problems and known errors to CIs, and uses the Configuration Management Database (CMDB) data to analyze incidents and problems. Verification of the actual configuration of the infrastructure against the authorized configuration in the CMDB can also identify deviations or defects in the infrastructure.
Change Management progresses the change request raised by Problem Management to remove known errors. Problem Management has to be informed about implementation of changes to identify and remedy any related problems.

Service Level Management
Service Level Management (SLM) uses information from Configuration Management about services, relationships between services and about the underlying infrastructure. The CMDB may also store SLM data and record the Service Level against the CIs (e.g. services, hardware, software).
Change Management uses information from Service Level Management to determine the impact of changes on services and business processes and to coordinate the planning of changes with the customer, where required. Change Management reports to Service Level Management in the form of a Projected Service Availability (PSA) report and lists the changes to agreed SLAs and the impact of the Forward Schedule of Changes (FSC) on the service availability.

Financial Management for IT Services

Financial Management uses Configuration Management information about the use of services and CIs (for example which department uses a processing service and who has a desktop PC and who a laptop). Combined with the information from the SLAs these details are used to determine the price to be charged. Financial Management also monitors IT components and investments (Asset Management).

Availability Management

Availability Management uses the CMDB for identifying the CIs, which contribute to a service, and for Component Failure Impact Analysis (CFIA). It draws up plans for changes to remove identified weaknesses. Configuration Management provides information about the composition of the chains of CIs on which the availability of services depend, as well as about each of the components.

Availability Management initiates changes that aim to improve service availability and will often be involved in estimating the potential impact of changes.

IT Service Continuity Management

IT Service Continuity Management uses standard configurations from the CMDB (baselines) to specify disaster recovery requirements and checks that these configurations are available at the disaster recovery site.

Change Management informs IT Service Continuity Management of all changes that could affect recovery plans.

Capacity Management

Capacity Management uses data from the CMDB to plan the optimization of the IT infrastructure, to allocate the workload and to develop a capacity plan.

Capacity Management is primarily concerned with the cumulative effect of changes over an extended period, such as an increase in response time and the need for more processing, network or storage capacity. Based on the Capacity Plan, Capacity Management and Change Management will propose enhancements and changes (via Requests for Change or RFCs) to improve use of existing capacity as well as to extend it.

4 Self Assessment

4.1 Introduction

The implementation or continual improvement of IT Service Management processes will need a clear view on the status of present qualities and performance. Self assessment will tell you how suitable your processes are, compared to your aims. These aims can be based on best practice advice like ITIL or any kind of maturity model, such as the Process Maturity Framework (PMF).

Only with the aid of the self-assessment can areas be identified where processes are weak or strong and prioritized actions be decided accordingly. Only with this methodical approach can a continual improvement be established over time.

4.2 Self-assessment methods

Before a self-assessment can be performed a decision will need to be made on the method to be used. This book gives only a brief overview of principle methods.

In general, an assessment can show how the process compares with

• the level of best practice you wanted to reach; and
• the level of maturity (within your selected framework) that you wanted to reach.

The most common assessments for best practice are found in the PD0015 self assessment workbook, which is based on ITIL and on the requirements detailed in the ISO 20000 standard. It contains about 350 questions, in a general section concerning IT Service Management, a section with high-level service management processes, and in questionnaires on each of the individual processes.

There are several Maturity Frameworks on the market, mostly based on or using the principles of the Capability Maturity Model (CMM), originally published by the Software Engineering Institute. But there are also other standards, including ISO 15504, PMF or CobiT.

CMM and ISO 15504 were originally designed for software development, but they are now also adapted for a wider range of applications. CobiT was established by the Information System Audit and Control Association (ISACA) as a control and management framework. The Process Maturity Framework for Service Management (PMF) is based on principles developed by the Harvard Business School and IBM in the 1970s. More details of this framework are listed in our 'Planning to Implement Service Management' publication.

CMM, ISO 15504, PMF and CobiT utilize a maturity model, including a detailed description of what is needed at each level of maturity. For CobiT a detailed questionnaire is available on the internet (ISACA website).

4.3   Achieving a self-assessment

Before starting an assessment, the following issues should be taken into consideration:
- If only a single process is assessed, high-level concerns like service management policies and identification of risk should be considered. This is because every process should follow an integrated approach to IT Service Management.
- For best results, questions must be answered accurately and objectively. Take care to include anyone who has helped to develop and sustain the process. It may be better to use a reviewer from a separate but related part of the organization, or an external consultant, to ensure an unbiased answer.
- Self-assessment should always be undertaken by two people, to avoid subjectivity. If two people are doing the assessment they may have to adjust their views accordingly, and the result is likely to be more objective.
- Assessment reports can often produce vast amounts of information, but the value of that data depends on how it is organized and interpreted. Therefore, sufficient knowledge on interpretation should be available, or an external consultant should assist the process.
- The results of the assessment must clearly display any gaps or shortcomings. The risks of not closing such gaps should be identified. The prioritizing of activities and the communication of all information should be handled in a clear way.

Activities to accomplish a self assessment:
- **Select the relevant candidates** - If you conduct an assessment you should not only interrogate the relevant process owners or managers, but also functional managers and any relevant staff who work with the processes which are being assessed.
- **Perform the inquiry** - While assessing, try to be as impartial as possible, and rate the questions honestly. There is no value in being biased or over- or under-rating, because the goal should be a representation of what really exists. If you selected a maturity based self-assessment, use the maturity definitions and activity descriptions as guides.
- **Review the results** - After conducting the assessment, the results should be analyzed to determine further actions. Decisions on priority should be based on what can be done and what needs to be done. Workshops focusing on discussion and brainstorming may help to identify the right actions.
- **Track the initiatives** - Use the Action Table to document your improvement priorities and progress. Make sure each initiative is given an owner, a timeframe and a validation metric (i.e. what it is that you need to see as evidence that the initiative is delivering benefits).

It is important that an action table is created and actively tracked. If a continual Service Quality Plan (SQP) is available, the activities from the assessment can be handled by this list.

Repeating the assessment after a fixed period (i.e. six or twelve months) or after all activities have been implemented should demonstrate a clear improvement of the IT Service Management.

5 Configuration Management

5.1 Introduction

Configuration Management is more than storing information into a database. The information must be needed, well organized and, of course, be up-to-date. Most, if not all organizations have many sources of information in many formats, ranging from sophisticated integrated IT Service Management tools, to in-house developed applications, to small database and spreadsheets.

So why is it so difficult to properly implement Configuration Management? Probably since, as indicated above, organizations have all this information, all over the place and often duplicated. What is missing is a way of managing and organizing this information into a coherent source of information. This is where the *process* of Configuration Management comes in.

5.1.1 Goal

The goal of Configuration Management is to provide information on a logical model of the infrastructure or a service by identifying, controlling, maintaining and verifying the versions of Configuration Items (CIs) in existence[1].

The main goals of the Configuration Management process are to:
• account for all the IT assets and configurations;
• provide accurate information on configurations and their documentation.

5.1.2 Scope

Configuration Management covers the identification, recording, and reporting of IT components, including their versions, status, constituent components and relationships[2].

As a basic rule, Configuration Management covers all components that are subject to Change Management: as a minimum this will include CIs like hardware, software and associated documentation, but it can also include network, facilities, and staff. Services, composed of these CIs, will be subject to both Change and Configuration management.

Not all items are potentially covered by Change and Configuration Management. Items that are normally out of scope, are:
• furniture such as desks, chairs, tables, filing cabinets;
• traditional corporate assets such as buildings, land, manufacturing equipment and accounts receivable and inventory.

A clarification must be made about inventory. Corporate inventory includes raw material, products being manufactured and finished products.

---

1   See also OGC's Service Support book section 7.1 Goal of Configuration Management
2   See also OGC's Service Support book section 7.2 Scope of Configuration Management

5.1.3   Basic concepts

Configuration Management Database
The Configuration Management Database (CMDB) will store all relevant information about IT components (Configuration Items - CIs) throughout their life cycle. The CMDB has to be based upon database technology that provides flexible and powerful interrogation facilities.

The CMDB holds CIs that are described with their attributes. The CMDB also holds information on the relationship with other items like changes and incidents, or with staff. If other corporate databases register these items for other purposes, a relation to these components can be sufficient. E.g. changes will most likely be registered in a Change Management database, so a relation between both databases would make change information available from each related CI. The Change Management database may hold a lot more information on these changes than relevant to this CI. The relationship to a staff database can make relevant staff information available for each CI: who is the responsible application manager for a given application, who is the system manager for a given system, who is the Service Manager, et cetera, and where can you reach them (location, team, phone, email). The Human Resource Manager will have much more information in his staff database, not relevant for the CI.

This way the CMDB can link up to other corporate databases. The demarcation line between the CMDB and other corporate databases is determined by the scope of IT Service Management. If each attribute of a staff member would be subject to Change Management, then the entire staff database would be part of the CMDB; Human Resource Management would then be completely subject to Service Management. Practice learns that only a minor part of the staff database is subject to Change Management (e.g. infrastructure management roles of staff), and that it is hard enough to manage even these parts.

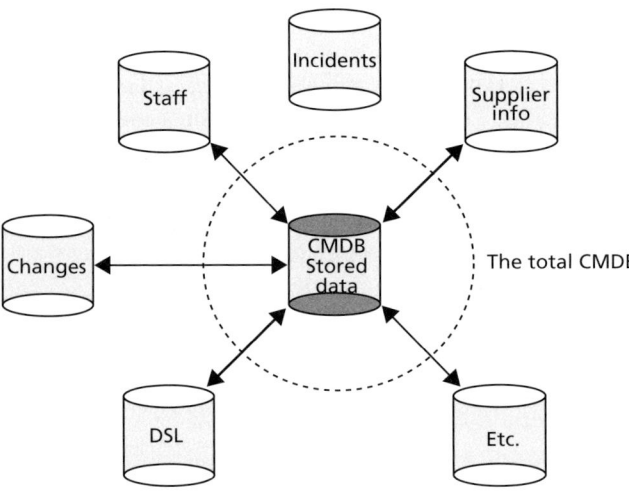

Figure 5.1   CMDB and relationships with other databases

The CMDB may be used to store some or all of the following:
- **Generic** - details of IT components such as location, owner, serial number, version number.
- **Class** - the type of component such as service, system, hardware, software, document, etc.
- **Financial** - initial cost, maintenance cost, spare parts, support costs, supplier, purchase date and renewal date for a license.
- **Record Trail** - who has updated the CI record, when, and what information is new or changed.
- **Relationship** - relationship information between CIs such as parent-child, peer-to-peer, is used by, uses, etc.
- **Historical** - relationships to associated incident, problem, known error, change and release records.

Software and document libraries

There are many types of software and associated documentation libraries. The access to these libraries should be restricted to those individuals and functional groups involved in the development, testing and implementation phases of a release. It is possible to provide access to the libraries for various support groups who may require to 're-install' defective software, or when a new desktop is required – in the case of desktop software and applications.

Document libraries are often known as knowledge bases or knowledge libraries. Access to the documents contained in those libraries should be restricted to read-only for most support staffs and end-users. Access rights and permissions make this relatively easy to implement.

The content of these libraries do not fall under the management of the Configuration Management process: each CI is managed by its respective process: a software version is managed by Change and Release Management, a document is managed by the process that uses the document. Configuration Management registers these items and their relationships, and makes sure the information on these items is available and reliable.

The **Definitive Software Library (DSL)** refers to the physical storage areas for the definitive authorized versions of all software CIs. A popular misconception is that Software CIs are stored in the CMDB. This is not the case. The CMDB contains a record of information about the software CI. The DSL holds the physical media used to store the software CI. There should be separate libraries for development, test and live filestore areas. The DSL itself is managed in the Release Management process.

The **Definitive Hardware Store (DHS)** is the term used for the secure storage of all hardware types in use. These spares are maintained at the same level as the equipment in the live environment. A popular misconception is that all spare parts are stored in the DHS. This is not the case. The DHS holds the authorized hardware configurations in use, to serve as 'templates' for rebuilding, or for the purpose of analysis in Incident or Problem Management. The DHS itself is managed in the Release Management process.

License Management

License Management is about monitoring and controlling the licenses acquired by an organization. Configuration Management will enable an organization to identify where unauthorized copies of licensed software are found. For example, an employee may hold a licensed copy of a particular software, but not be authorized to have it on his desktop.

License Management will also enable an organization to track illegally downloaded and installed software.

There are different software license structures such as individual, corporate and multi-licensing schemes. Senior managers are liable to face imprisonment and fines if illegal software is found to be in use within their enterprise.

Configuration baseline
A configuration baseline is the current configuration of a configuration item (logical or physical) defined at a specific point in time. The baseline records the structure and the details of a configuration. The purpose of a baseline is to act as a reference for further activities such as indicating growth, recovery from a failure or crisis. It can also be used as an upper limit. For example, a new version of an operating system is now available, but the organization has decided that it will not use it yet, nor develop or acquire applications based on this new operating system. A configuration baseline is normally stored in the DHS.

5.1.4   Roles and Responsibilities of Configuration Management[3]
The following roles may be considered. A detailed description of these roles can be found in the section "Tips & Templates" at the end of this chapter.
*   **Configuration Manager,** responsible for organizing and managing the Configuration Management process;
*   **Configuration Librarian,** responsible for the operational activities of the Configuration Management process.

5.2   Topics & theory 'Manage'
The typical management activities of a practitioner Configuration Management would be:
*   Plan the key activities in the Configuration Management process.
*   Plan the exchange of appropriate information on managing the Configuration Management process.
*   Report on the effectiveness and efficiency of the activities within the Configuration Management process.

5.2.1   Plan the key activities
The 'managing' activity is not part of the process design and implementation. At this stage, the process is established, roles are assigned, procedures in existence, the tool in place and populated. The activity focuses on managing 'who, what, where, when, and how' the process activities are to be carried out.
We should first revisit the main Configuration Management process activities.

Configuration Management planning
Configuration Management planning consists of agreeing and defining:
1. **The strategy, policy, scope and objectives of Configuration Management.**
    The managing activity uses the above as a guide to determine if the activities are to be conducted, if the CIs are within the current scope of Configuration Management and which objectives are to be reported against.

---
3   Adapted from Annex 7B: Specific responsibilities of the Configuration Management team in the OGC's Service Support book

2. **The analysis of the current position of assets and configurations.**

   The managing activity uses the current position as a starting guide to determine when to verify, what to control, what to record and to determine gaps in the information stored in the CMDB.

3. **The organizational context, both technical and managerial, within which the Configuration Management activities are to be implemented.**

   The managing activity looks at the current organizational structure, the roles and responsibilities of the various support groups involved in the process of Configuration Management. It is important to understand the culture of the organization. Implementing formal processes within an organization changes the culture of the organization to a certain degree, but implementing many processes may have an even greater effect.

   It is also required to look at the organization itself. Is it a distributed environment? How old or new is the infrastructure? What are the languages involved? How much outsourcing is taking place currently? What are the issues, challenges and projects affecting the organization today? Is there a merger, acquisition, legislation or the launch of a new product on the event horizon?

4. **The policies for related processes such as Change Management and Release Management.**

   The managing activity looks closely at the current state of the Change and Release Management processes to ensure that the appropriate touch points are identified and that the proper exchange of information happens, based on the current and possibly upcoming state of the organization and the technology. What is the current maturity of the processes involved? Are the processes deployed to the whole organization or to limited areas? This would have an impact on the policies regulating the relationships between the processes.

5. **Interfaces (e.g. between projects, suppliers, application and support teams).**

   There are primarily five roles within an IT department. They are *design and planning*, *deployment*, *operations*, *technical support* and *development*. While functional teams fall within one of these primary roles, processes span multiple roles. Procedures will have to identify the proper target audience in order to ensure that they are executed by the right groups at the right time. It will also be imperative to align the individual Key Performance Indicators to those of procedures and processes in order to achieve greater buy-in from the rank and file.

6. **The relevant processes, procedures, guidelines, support tools, roles, authorities and responsibilities for each of the Configuration Management activities.**

   Configuration Management activities can easily be perceived as administrative and not really necessary right now. The attitude of "I'll get to it later" must not be tolerated. It will be important to sell the benefits of properly executing the activities of Configuration Management to all interested parties. To ensure that procedures are properly executed, policies must first be defined and agreed. These policies will then provide guidance as to why the procedures must be properly executed.

The next step will be to explain the authority matrix that defines the roles and responsibilities of everyone concerned with the Configuration Management process. The authority matrix will explain who has overall accountability for the process, who is responsible for the proper execution of the activities and procedures, who can be consulted when in doubt and who must be kept informed and why.

Configuration identification and CIs

The managing activity determines when information about a CI needs to be entered in the CMDB, based on the touch points with other processes such as Change and Release Management. It is important to know *when* to trigger the identification activity, *who* will execute it, *what* needs to be identified and labeled, *how* to identify the information, *how* to label, etc.

Correct configuration identification and documentation enables Change Management to be effective by fully recognizing the potential impact of a particular change.

Configuration control

The managing activity determines the level of control given to anyone who will be accessing the CMDB and why. This activity must continuously ensure that not only the right amount of control is provided, but that it is properly communicated, especially to those new to the process. Configuration control is concerned with ensuring that only authorized and identifiable CIs are recorded from receipt to disposal. It ensures that no CI is added, modified, replaced or removed without appropriate controlling documentation e.g. an approved change request.

Configuration control usually defines only a few people who can update the CMDB. Configuration control also sees to a proper procedures on the information that has to be delivered by Release and Change Management. Especially when third parties are involved the procedures must be tight. The appropriate timing for administration issues has to be set as well, so all parties will get the right information at the right time.

Configuration status accounting

The managing activity is concerned with determining when to provide status accounting reports, and to whom to provide the reports. For this, it is important to understand the life cycle of each type of component and to plan appropriately. Status accounting is very dependent on the previous two activities, identification and control. Without these activities, the status accounting will be deficient at best. Figure 5.2 shows an example of a life cycle and additional statusses.

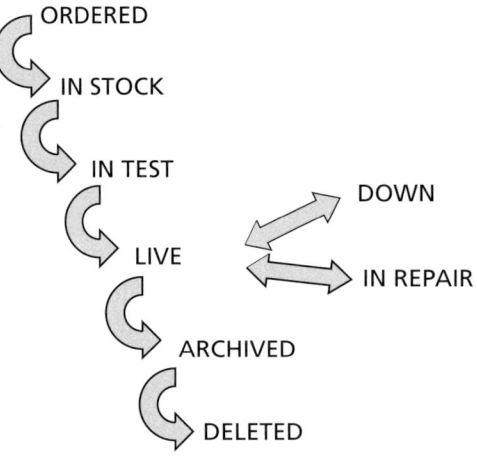

Figure 5.2   Example of life cycle stages and additional statusses

After withdrawal or deletion of a CI, it may be required to store historic data for some time, depending on the items or on the line of business. E.g. in pharmaceutical business a company may be required to reproduce the manufacturing process of a drug after 20 years, which clearly has effects on the IT systems used for that process.

The Service Desk has to be informed of updated the CI status when Release Management has distributed a release. This means that the status of CIs has to be changed on the agreed time.

Configuration verification and audit
The managing activity must plan ahead when verification is to be conducted and why. Appropriate procedures must be in place. Configuration verification and audit comprises a series of reviews and audits that verify the physical existence of CIs, and check that the CIs are correctly recorded in the CMDB and controlled libraries. It includes the verification of release and configuration documentation before changing the live environment.
It has to be determined how urgent verifications are, and whether the verification has to be done at regular intervals, or on specific times, or only when time allows. The Service Desk might be of assistence in occasional audits, because they have frequent contact with the users.

5.2.2   Plan the exchange of appropriate management information
The managing activity also looks at determining the appropriate exchange of information between the various processes. In this case, Configuration Management must plan the information that it requires from Change and Release Management, and when it will need this information. In addition, Configuration Management must plan the information it must provide in return to the Change and Release Management processes. Of course, Configuration Management provides information to all other processes, to the business and also to vendors, but these are beyond the scope of this discussion. Some examples of relationship between Configuration Management and the other processes are provided at the end of this chapter.

It is important when designing process flows and procedures to identify the inputs and outputs of each activity. It must be noted that the source of the inputs and the destination of the outputs must also be provided. Some outputs will remain within the procedure or the activity or even the process, and become inputs into the next activity, but many outputs must be provided to the other processes.
In essence, the managing activity plans for the success of the process by ensuring that everything is in place, in working condition, that roles and responsibilities are defined, that tools are in place and that the exchange of information takes place.

5.2.3   Report on the effectiveness and efficiency of the activities
The effectiveness of Configuration Management can be demonstrated by its Critical Success Factors (CSFs) and Key Performance Indicators (KPIs). In regards to Configuration Management, effectiveness may - for example - be demonstrated by fewer errors or omissions in the CMDB month over month, while efficiency may be demonstrated by taking less time to perform an audit (while still doing it properly) month over month.

Of course, Configuration Management does not happen in isolation and its relationship to other processes such as Change and Release Management can not be ignored. The effectiveness and efficiency of any of the Release & Control processes will be dependent on the effectiveness and efficiency of the other two processes. This is why it is recommended to report on the effectiveness of the Release & Control processes instead of any process by itself.

5.3   Topics & theory 'Organize'

The typical organizing activities of a practitioner Configuration Management would be:
- Organize the exchange of appropriate configuration information with other processes.
- Provide configuration information to other IT Service Management processes, users and suppliers.
- Maintain the procedures of the Configuration Management process.
- Maintain the baselines of configurations and status information of Configuration Items.
- Monitor CI logistics for releases (referring to CI status: purchase or develop internally, storage, transport, delivery, implementation).

5.3.1   Organize the exchange of appropriate configuration information with other processes

Organizing the exchange of information between processes is a key activity of any process. While managing refers to planning how each activity would be done, organizing is about actually doing the activities. There are three major areas to look at here. The first is to provide information to other processes in the form of reports. The second is to provide information in the form of access to the data, while the third is to receive the information from the other processes.

Providing access to the data must be controlled. This is where the control activity of Configuration Management comes in. There are many layers of access to a database:
- The ability to only read a record.
- The ability to create a new record.
- The ability to update an existing record.
- The ability to delete an existing record.
- The ability to archive an existing record.

Reports can be provided at many intervals for many reasons. The intervals include: daily, weekly, monthly, quarterly, annually and, of course, ad-hoc. There are four primary reasons to report. They are to justify, direct, intervene and to validate.

The following represents a sample of the information provided between Configuration Management (CFG) and Change Management (CHG):
- CFG provides CI attributes to assist in change assessment.
- CFG provides CI relationships to assist in change impact analysis.
- CFG provides CHG access to the CMDB to read CI information.
- CFG provides CHG with the ability to link change records to CI records.
- CHG provides CFG with feedback on incorrect or missing CI information.
- CHG provides CFG with new CI status.
- CHG provides CFG with ad-hoc verification on CI information.
- CHG provides CFG with feedback on CI level and scope.

The following represents a sample of the information provided between Configuration Management (CFG) and Release Management (REL):

- CFG provides CI attributes to assist in planning releases.
- CFG provides CI relationships to assist in building releases.
- CFG provides REL access to the CMDB to read CI information.
- CFG provides REL with the ability to link releases to CI records.
- CFG provides REL with inventory of the DSL.
- CFG provides REL with inventory of the DHS.
- REL provides CFG with feedback on incorrect or missing CI information.
- REL provides CFG with new CI status.
- REL provides CFG with ad-hoc verification on CI information.
- REL provides CFG with feedback on CI level and scope.

5.3.2 Provide configuration information to other IT Service Management processes, users and suppliers.

The following is a list of some of the reports that can be provided to the other processes, as well as to the customers, users and suppliers. While not exhaustive, this list provides a clue that many of the reports will be used for a variety of reasons by various other processes and functions. It is important to consider that information, although useful, can be overwhelming at times. It is not only useful to ask what information should be provided, but what will be done with that information.

Again, there are three major areas to look at here. The first is to provide information to other processes in the form of reports. The second is to provide information in the form of access to the data, while the third is to receive the information from the other processes.

Generic information from Configuration Management that can be provided to other processes and functions includes:

- Periodic statistical and analytical (weekly, monthly, quarterly) configuration reports, broken down by
  - new CI;
  - retired CI;
  - incorrect CI information;
  - status;
  - time and material used to execute the process.
- Process documentation such as process flows, procedures for various activities;
- Process tool documentation such as forms, work instructions
  - registration/logging of CI;
  - verification and audit reports with action items;
  - performing various activities of the CFG process.
- Process roles and responsibilities such as
  - Configuration Manager;
  - Configuration Librarian;
- Process documentation such as definitions of naming conventions, CI labeling, attributes, relationships, statuses;
- Process documentation such as relationships with other processes such as Change and Release Management;

- Documentation pertaining to the access to the CMDB;
- Process review documentation for continual improvement.

Please see the relationship section at the end of this chapter for further examples of the information provided between Configuration Management and the other Service Management processes.

5.3.3 Maintain the procedures of the Configuration Management process

Regardless of the process, it is important to always maintain the procedures and to ensure that other documentation is up-to-date. This should not be done on a daily basis, but should have been planned already through the managing activity. The intent of maintaining the procedures is not part of the optimizing activity but compliments and supports that activity.

First a procedure template is required, and also a feedback mechanism for when a procedure is discovered which is incomplete or erroneous. Someone can not simply modify a procedure whilst validating the fault. The principles of Incident Management and Change Management apply here. Why? Because procedures are documents and documents are CIs and therefore subject to any policy, process and procedure governing configuration items.
A pitfall in procedures is always the bureaucracy: the balance between dull and exciting work has to be observed here!

This means that when a fault is discovered in a procedure, it should be treated the same as an incident, and if a change is required then it is subject to the Change Management process. Of course the change may be a pre-approved standard change, but this may not necessarily be the case. It must be noted that the change, if any, must be documented and communicated to the appropriate parties.

Tip on identifying faults: Give the procedure manual to new employees and ask them to highlight any perceived discrepancy or faults. Then, with the assistance of a more experienced employee, go through the highlights and identify all real faults whilst explaining the misconceptions to the new employees. The result is a much improved procedure manual and better trained new employees.

Maintaining procedures is not only about finding faults, it is also about communication, education and training. The procedures must be communicated to the people who will be executing them. There must be an education component, such as roles and responsibilities, reason for the procedures, expected inputs and outputs, triggers, etc. Finally, training must take place so that employees will be able to properly execute the procedure and also to ensure greater buy-in into the new process.

5.3.4 Maintain the baselines of configurations and status information of Configuration Items

A configuration baseline may be created for any or all of the following reasons:
- as a sound basis for future work (e.g. a point in the life of a CI from which you can progress, such as an 'accepted' application);
- as a record of what CIs were affected by an RFC and what CIs were actually changed;
- as a point you can fall back to if things go wrong.

Since configuration baselines should be established by formal agreement at specific points in time and used as departure points for the formal control of a configuration, it is important not only to plan for them but to execute and document them appropriately. Configuration baselines plus approved changes to those baselines together constitute the currently approved configuration.

It is important to remember that baselines should be treated like CIs. They have to be properly identified, controlled and communicated. The activities of identification, control and status accounting will be key roles in establishing a baseline.
Of course the other Release & Control processes will provide the mechanism to trigger when a new baseline is to be taken. A baseline should not only be taken at regular intervals but also, for example, before and after major changes and releases.

For the three paragraphs below, the following applies:
The organizing activity of Configuration Management will be able to provide the instructions for designing, building and configuring releases strictly from a provider point of view, provided the procedures exist in the first place. The CMDB will contain records referencing where to find the information with the document libraries holding the actual procedures. The procedures will be either in hard or soft copy form.
Should new instructions be required, then Configuration Management will identify them, apply naming conventions, label them and record them in the CMDB. It will then store the documents in a document library.

Provide information for designing, building and configuring releases
Configuration Management will also provide the relationships between components. Configuration Management will provide this information so that Change and Release Management will be in a position to properly identify the impact of changes and releases as well as providing insight into the design, build and configuration of releases.
Configuration Management will also provide baseline information to assist change and Release Management.

Provide information for back-out and test plans for changes and releases
By providing the relationships between components, Configuration Management will enable Change and Release Management to properly identify the impact of changes and releases as well as providing the processes with insight into backing out and testing changes and releases.

Provide information to plan the implementation of releases
The relationship information from Configuration Management will enable Change and Release Management to properly identify the impact of changes and releases as well as providing insight into the implementation of releases.

Configuration Management will also provide baseline information to assist Change and Release Management in creating an inventory to the components to be deployed, retired, removed, etc. Configuration Management will provide location information so that releases can be implemented effectively.

In return, Release Management will provide Configuration Management with a list of deployed locations as part of a roll-out, and with missed areas, for example where automation has failed to push/pull and install new software.

5.3.5   Monitor CI logistics for changes and releases (CI status)

Configuration Management will monitor CI logistics for changes and releases: purchased or developed internally, storage, transport, delivery, implementation. For this particular activity, Configuration Management will use identification, control and status accounting to assist Change and Release Management in monitoring the logistics for each release. Organizing will involve a close working relationship between all three Release & Control processes. It is very likely that a single individual will perform the activities of multiple processes. This would make sense. The role of the Configuration Librarian will often be used to add these tasks to. See the role description of the Configuration Librarian at the end of this chapter.

In order to be successful in monitoring the logistics of a release, it will be important to have identified all the touch points between the *Change Management* activities and the identification, control and status accounting activities of Configuration Management. This is demonstrated in figure 5.3.

To complete the Release & Control cycle with regard to the monitoring of the logistics of a change or a release, it will be important to have identified all the touch points between the *Release Management* activities and the identification, control and status accounting activities of Configuration Management. This is illustrated in figure 5.4.

5.4   Topics & theory 'Optimize'

The key optimizing activities of a practitioner Configuration Management would be to:
• monitor and optimize the Configuration Management process;
• propose improvements, based on results of monitoring and reviews;
• plan and conduct configuration audits and reviews.

5.4.1   Monitor and optimize the Configuration Management process

In order to optimize anything it is imperative that goals were originally set. These goals, as mentioned previously in chapter 2, must follow the SMART approach. The question then becomes what do you want or need to be monitored in order to optimize it?
First it is important to follow a measuring process. A simple measuring process consists of gathering, processing, analyzing and using the data. This measuring process may look simplistic at first but it is actually quite complex as it requires both automation and human intervention. There are plenty of monitoring tools available today but it is a major drawback that they can collect (gather) all kinds of data points. There is often too much data to manage. This is not to say that tools are bad. Far from it! But too many organizations have badly implemented monitoring tools without first understanding why they want to monitor in the first place.

Going back to the CSF and KPI discussion earlier in the chapter we get our starting point. One of the managing activities is to 'Report on the effectiveness and efficiency of the activities

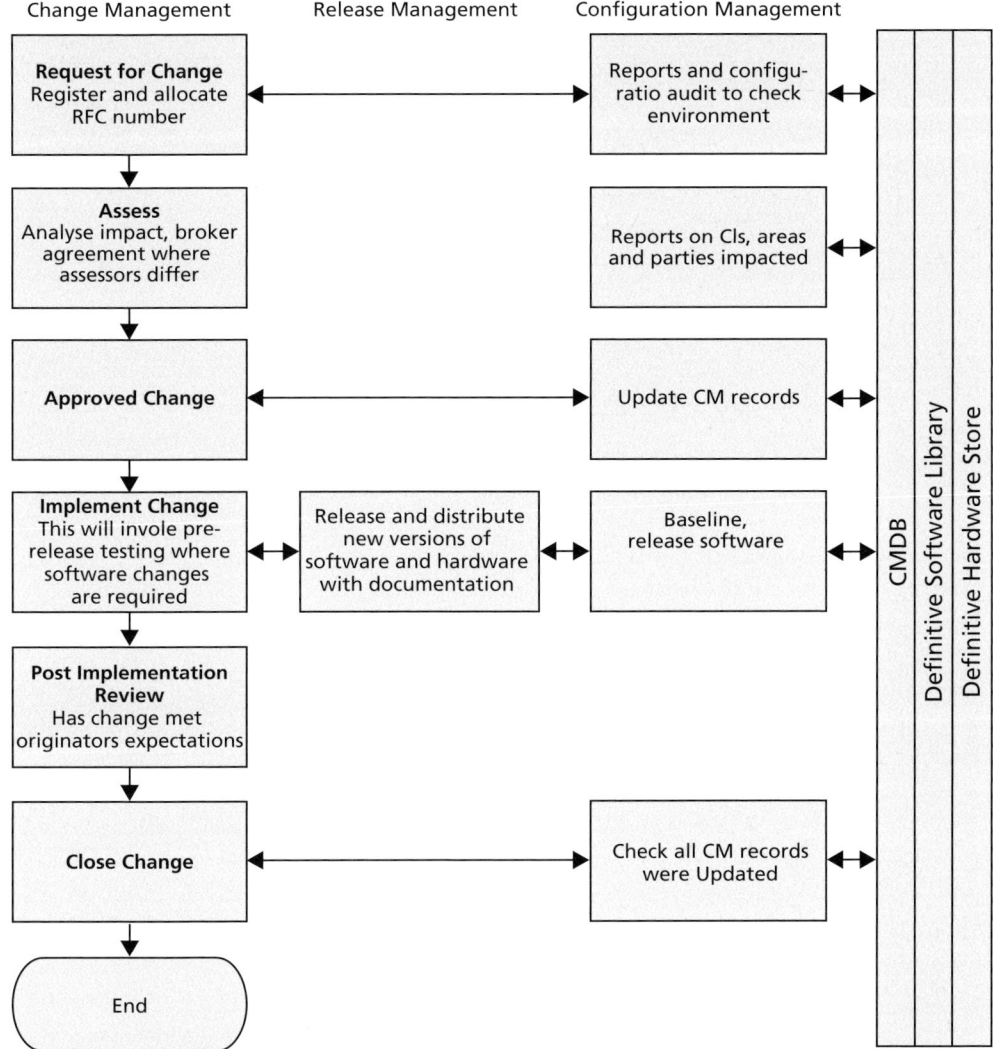

Figure 5.3   Relationship between Configuration, Change and Release Management (based on: OGC, Service Support)

within the Configuration Management process'. Therefore one must define what is meant by effectiveness and efficiency.

KPIs are usually expressed in terms of an increase or decrease of a percentage of something over a period of time. Here is an example:

A 10 per cent decrease in the number of incorrectly recorded CIs over the next 6 months.

In this case, how do we set up the monitoring and optimizing?
• Identify a sample set of CIs to be monitored.
• Establish the current baseline of this sample set of CIs.
• Physically verify each CI in the sample set.
• Compare the baseline with the verification report.

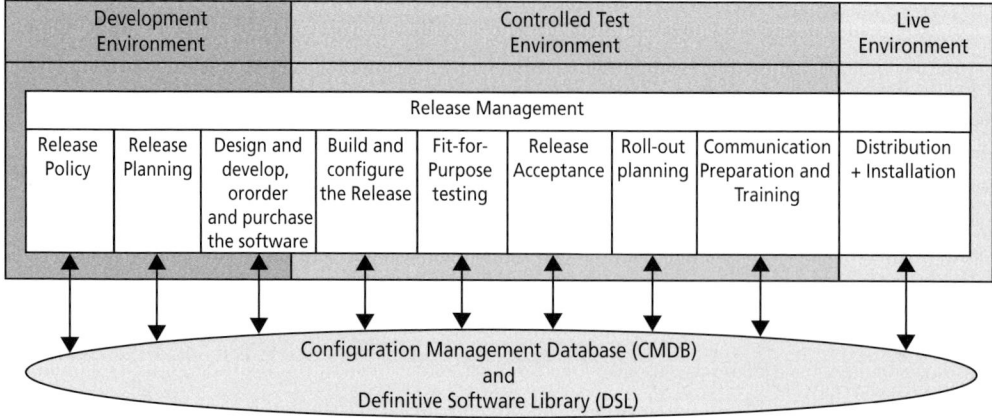

Development Environment			Controlled Test Environment						Live Environment
Release Management									
Release Policy	Release Planning	Design and develop, ororder and purchase the software	Build and configure the Release	Fit-for-Purpose testing	Release Acceptance	Roll-out planning	Communication Preparation and Training		Distribution + Installation

Configuration Management Database (CMDB)
and
Definitive Software Library (DSL)

Figure 5.4   Major activities in Release Management (Source: OGC, Service Support)

- Identify and document any and all discrepancies.
- Find the reason for the discrepancies.
- Identify and document the reasons for the discrepancies. This will be useful in the next activity 'Proposing improvements …'
- Make some recommendations, apply the recommendations and repeat at regular intervals, say every two months since the example indicates a six months period.
- Look for trends in the right direction.

In this example, we only looked at one aspect of one process. There are many other aspects of the Configuration Management process that can be optimized. Which ones to choose? Go back to your goals and objectives. Look at the CSFs and KPIs. This will guide and influence your monitoring activities. Again, no more than two or three CSFs should be considered at any given time and no more than two or three KPIs per CSF. This represents between four and nine KPIs for one process, in this case, Configuration Management.

One of the major errors that people make is to only concentrate on what is being monitored. It is important to ensure constant buy-in into the process and to look at all aspects of Configuration Management; the process, the technology and the people. It is possible that the process works well and that the technology is more than adequate. Still something may not be right. What about the people? It is important, not only to modify and update procedure and to adjust the tools via maintenance and upgrades, but to optimize the people through communication, education and training as well.

It is also important to look at job description, performance appraisals, education and training aids. By adding the human element to the monitoring activity, the picture becomes a lot more complicated as it requires manual observation, discussions, forums and the like. This also requires more time and it can only be automated to a certain extent.

5.4.2 Propose improvements, based on results of monitoring and reviews

In the previous activity it was mentioned that the reasons for discrepancies would be useful here, by analyzing the reasons and by proposing improvements. Again all aspects of the process must be considered; process, people and technology. Furthermore, a *cost benefit analysis* of the proposed improvement must be conducted and provided. Coming up with a million dollar solution for a ten thousand dollar issue is not very cost effective, whilst proposing a ten thousand dollar improvement to a million dollar issue is a lot more cost effective.

In essence, when proposing improvements, use Problem Management to identify the component at fault, the workaround, the permanent solution and then submit a Request for Change (RFC). The change (the proposed improvement) goes through the Change Management process just like any other change/improvement request.

Planned reviews normally result in a discrepancies report. This report can show the following kinds of discrepencies (Table 5.1):
- **A CI was registered in the CMDB but not found in practice.** Possible explanations and improvement actions can be:
  - the CI was stolen. Possible action: forward an RFC for a new CI.
  - the CI was moved. Possible action: forward an RFC for a move of the CI to its official position, or forward an RFC to legitimize the current position of the CI.
- **A CI was registered in the CMDB but found differently in practice.** Possible explanations and improvement actions can be:
  - the CI was changed without involving Change Management. Possible action: forward an RFC to change the CI back to its official configuration, or to ligitimize its current configuration.
  - the CI was changed, involving Change Management, but the change was not registered. Possible action: register the CI's actual configuration. Check how the registration could have been missed in the Change Management process.
  - the CI was changed, involving Change Management, but the change was not yet registered. This indicates a backlog. Possible action: add more resources to the registration responsibility, or influence work priorities.
- **A CI was found in practice but not registered in the CMDB.** Possible explanations and improvement actions can be:
  - the CI was installed without forwarding an RFC. Possible action: remove or legitimize the CI through an RFC. This could be the illegal move, mentioned above.
  - the CI was installed in a regular change, but not registered or not yet registered. Possible action: see above.
- **A CI was found in practice but registered differently in the CMDB. Possible explanations and improvement actions can be:**
  - the CI was changed without forwarding an RFC. Possible action: change the CI back to its original configuration or ligitimize the current configuration through an RFC.
  - the CI was changed in a regular change, but not registered or not yet registered. Possible action: see above.

Discrepancies report	CI registered in CMDB	CI not registered in CMDB
CI found in practice	good!	check situation and take action!
CI not found in practice	check situation and take action!	non-issue

Table 5.1   Possible discrepancies, to be found in a configuration review

The review/audit can show process compliance issues: the Identification and Configuration Control and Status Accounting procedures are not followed correctly.

Process Compliance issues may be attributed to, but not limited to, one of the following:
- unauthorized changes;
- non-adherence to the process;
- undocumented incident resolution;
- incorrectly documented releases;
- role misinterpretation.

Process Quality: Imperfections in the Configuration, Change, Incident, and Release Management process. The interfaces between the Change, Incident, and Release Management processes with the Configuration Management process itself do not function properly.

Process Performance: The process is functional, but does not meet the performance requirements due to work load or lack of knowledge in the process.
Depending on the cause of the exception, an improvement plan must be initiated. The improvement plan can involve re-instructing process workers, revising existing procedures and work instructions, or redefining interfaces with other processes.

The discrepancy will be one of the following items:
- RFC (In Progress)
- Process deficiency
  - Compliance
  - Quality
  - Performance

In all cases disciplinary measures can be taken, based on the findings in the review, or education can be planned to prevent the situation from happening again. These actions are then in fact part of the Problem Management process.

5.4.3 Plan and conduct configuration audits and reviews

Proposals for improvements must be planned ahead of time and should not be solely triggered by a major crisis. As part of any good process design, a review is already scheduled at regular intervals based on the CSFs and the KPIs. All three major components are reviewed: process, people and technology.

Identifying the requirements for a review/audit includes the following triggers:
- Schedule
- Problem Management trend
- Major release
- Financial auditing
- Acquisition/sale
- Corrupted CMDB

The scope and scale of the review must also be identified, together with the baseline for the sample set of components.

The next step is to plan the review/audit. This includes:
- **Who** - who will do the review/audit;
- **What** – what is the scale/scope;
- **Where** - the locations that will be reviewed;
- **When** – schedule the review;
- **How** - manual and/or auto-discovery.

5.5 Relationships

5.5.1 General
Configuration Management is an integral part of all other Service Management processes. With current, accurate and comprehensive information about all components in the infrastructure, the management of change, in particular, is more effective and efficient. Change Management can be integrated with Configuration Management as much as possible.
The CMDB should be made available to the entire Service Support group and other groups, e.g. Service Management, so that incidents and problems can be resolved more easily by understanding the possible cause of the failing component.

Configuration Management is heavily dependent upon a number of other disciplines. Effective Change Management, Release Management and its activities: Software Control, Distribution, coordination of Acceptance Testing, and procedures for the installation and acceptance of new/different hardware and network components are all essential. If these are not already in existence, they should be planned alongside Configuration Management.

5.5.2 Interfaces with other IT Service Management processes

CFG	=	Configuration Management
CI	=	Configuration Management
CMDB	=	Configuration Management DataBase
IM	=	Incident Management
PM	=	Problem Management
REL	=	Release Management
SLM	=	Service Level Management
AVM	=	Availability Management
CAP	=	Capacity Management
ITSCM	=	IT Service Continuity Management
FM	=	Financial Management

Incident Management
1. CFG provides information on CI attributes to assist in incident investigation.
2. CFG provides information on CI relationships to assist in incident classification.
3. CFG provides IM access to the CMDB to read CI information.

4. CFG provides IM with the ability to link incident records to CI records.
5. IM provides CFG with feedback on incorrect or missing CI information.
6. IM provides CFG with new CI status.
7. IM provides CFG with ad-hoc verification on CI information.
8. IM provides CFG with feedback on CI level and scope.

Problem Management
1. CFG provides information on CI attributes to assist in problem investigation.
2. CFG provides information on CI relationships to assist in problem classification.
3. CFG provides PM access to the CMDB to read CI information.
4. CFG provides PM with the ability to link problem records to CI records.
5. PM provides CFG with feedback on incorrect or missing CI information.
6. PM provides CFG with new CI status.
7. PM provides CFG with ad-hoc verification on CI information.
8. PM provides CFG with feedback on CI level and scope.

Service Level Management
1. SLM provides CFG with the service attributes to track.
2. SLM provides all relevant documentation to be tracked in the CMDB.
3. SLM provides SLA structure to assist in the design of the CMDB data structure.
4. CFG provides SLM with the relationships between service CIs.
5. CFG provides naming conventions for service CIs.
6. CFG provides verification and audit reports to SLM.
7. CFG provides status accounting reports to SLM.

Availability Management
1. CFG provides AVM with information on the relationships between CIs to assist in conducting a Component Failure Impact Analysis (CFIA).
2. CFG provides AVM with information on the relationships between CIs to assist in conducting a Fault Tree Analysis (FTA).
3. CFG provides AVM with information on the relationships between CIs to assist in conducting a Service Outage Analysis (SOA).
4. CFG provides AVM with information on the relationships between CIs to assist in conducting a risk analysis.
5. CFG provides naming conventions for service CIs.
6. CFG provides verification and audit reports to AVM.
7. CFG provides status accounting reports to AVM.
8. CFG provides AVM with access to the CMDB to synchronize the information in the Availability Management Database (AMDB).
9. AVM provides a completed CFIA to assist in identifying correct or updated CI relationships.
10. AVM provides a completed FTA to assist in identifying correct or updated CI relationships.
11. AVM provides a completed SOA to assist in identifying correct or updated CI relationships.
12. AVM provides all relevant documentation to be tracked in the CMDB.

13. AVM provides CFG with access to the AMDB to synchronize the information in the CMDB.

Capacity Management
1. CFG provides CAP with information on the relationships between CIs to assist in conducting application sizing.
2. CFG provides CAP with information on the relationships between CIs to assist in conducting modeling methods.
3. CFG provides CAP with information on the relationships between CIs to assist in establish workload balancing.
4. CFG provides CAP with information on CIs and their relationships to assist in establishing Demand Management.
5. CFG provides naming conventions for service CIs.
6. CFG provides verification and audit reports to CAP.
7. CFG provides status accounting reports to CAP.
8. CFG provides CAP with access to the CMDB to synchronize the information in the CDB.
9. CAP provides completed modeling reports to assist in identifying correct or updated CI relationships.
10. CAP provides all relevant documentation to be tracked in the CMDB.
11. CAP provides CFG with access to the CDB to synchronize the information in the CMDB.

IT Service Continuity Management
1. CFG provides ITSCM with information on the relationships between CIs to assist in conducting Business Impact Analysis (BIA).
2. CFG provides ITSCM with information on the relationships between CIs to assist in conducting Risk analysis.
3. CFG provides ITSCM with information on the relationships between CIs to assist in establishing counter-measures.
4. CFG provides ITSCM with information on the relationships between CIs to assist in analyzing a crisis before invoking an ITSCM plan.
5. CFG provides naming conventions for service CIs.
6. CFG provides verification and audit reports to ITSCM.
7. CFG provides status accounting reports to ITSCM.
8. ITSCM provides all relevant documentation to be tracked in the CMDB.

Financial Management
1. CFG provides FM with information on the financial CI attributes to assist in budgeting.
2. CFG provides FM with information on the financial CI attributes to assist in accounting for IT services.
3. CFG provides FM with information on the financial CI attributes to assist in charging.
4. CFG provides naming conventions for service CIs
5. CFG provides verification and audit reports to FM.
6. CFG provides status accounting reports to FM.
7. FM provides all relevant documentation to be tracked in the CMDB.
8. FM provides cost models to assist CFG in tracking relevant FM attributes.

9. FM provides CFG with budgeting templates and attributes to assist CFG in budgeting for its activities.
10. FM provides CFG with budgeting templates and attributes to assist CFG in accounting for its activities.

5.5.3 Interface with Security Management

Security Management (SEC)
1. CFG provides SEC with information on the CI attributes to assist in planning for security.
2. CFG provides SEC with information on the CI relationships to assist in planning for security.
3. CFG provides SEC with access to the CMDB.
4. CFG provides naming conventions for service CIs.
5. CFG provides verification and audit reports to SEC.
6. CFG provides status accounting reports to SEC.
7. SEC provides all relevant documentation to be tracked in the CMDB.
8. SEC provides security policy to assist CFG in tracking relevant SEC attributes.
9. SEC provides guidelines to assist CFG in providing access to the CMDB to the appropriate people.

5.6 About Tools

5.6.1 Data ownership models (centralized, distributed, federated, etc.)

In IT Service Management, databases are perceived at a conceptual level. This goes for all IT Service Management databases and for the CMDB in particular. For the physical representation of the CMDB you can think of one central database, but it could also be several local copies of databases that get harmonized with tools that are only known to the Configuration Manager.

For example we can distinguish a CMDB from an incident database and a problem database. These could however be one physical database in a tool you are using. Is this wrong? No! IT Service Management is concerned with the level where technology is not yet plugged in. And there are three logical conceptual different databases in the example. It is not important whether technology makes one big physical database of them, or not. So the basic knowledge of databases should come in handy for a Configuration Manager, but the technical knowledge could be somewhere else, as long as the tool-provider in your IT department builds the databases you need.

Conclusion: think of databases not as a physical object but in a conceptual or logical way.

Note: Closer to the technology this view will fade from logical to technical. When we talk about back-up of the CMDB, we ARE talking about the physical thing of course, but we are not interested in back-up technology[4].

---

4   Source: "Databaseontwerp, van informatiemodel naar databaseschema" by Pollaert, Van Eeden & Kranenburg; Publisher: Thema, Netherlands, ISBN 90.5871.115.3

5.6.2 Tools

Configuration Management system

The Configuration Management system should prevent changes from being made to an IT infrastructure without valid authorization via Change Management. The authorization record should automatically 'drive' the change. The Configuration Management system should:

- provide sufficient security controls to limit access on a need-to-know basis;
- provide support for CIs of varying complexity, e.g. entire systems, releases, single hardware items, software modules, or hierarchic and networked relationships between CIs; by holding information on the relationships between CIs, Configuration Management tools facilitate the impact assessment of RFCs;
- provide easy addition of new CIs and deletion of old CIs;
- provide automatic validation of input data (e.g. are all CI names unique);
- provide automatic establishment of all relationships that can be automatically established, when new CIs are added;
- provide support for CIs with different model numbers, version numbers, and copy numbers;
- provide automatic identification of other affected CIs when any CI is the subject of an incident report/record, problem record, known error record or RFC;
- provide integration of Problem Management data within the CMDB, or at least an interface from the Configuration Management system to any separate Problem Management databases that may exist;
- provide automatic updating and recording of the version number of a CI if the version number of any component CI is changed;
- provide maintenance of a history of all CIs (both a historical record of the current version - such as installation date, records of changes, previous locations, etc - and of previous versions);
- provide support for the management and use of configuration baselines (corresponding to definitive copies, versions, etc.), including support for reversion to trusted versions;
- provide ease of interrogation of the CMDB and good reporting facilities, including trend analysis (e.g. the ability to identify the number of RFCs affecting particular CIs);
- provide ease of reporting of the CI inventory so as to facilitate configuration audits;
- provide flexible reporting tools to facilitate impact analyses;
- provide the ability to show graphically the configuration or network maps of interconnected CIs, and to input information about new CIs via such maps;
- provide the ability to show the hierarchy of relationships between 'parent' CIs and 'child' CIs.

Change Management and Release Management support

To support Change Management and Release Management, the Configuration Management tools should provide automated support for the following:

- identification of related CIs affected by a proposed change to assist with impact assessment;
- recording of CIs that are affected by authorized changes;
- Implementation of changes including package releases in accordance with authorization records;
- registering of CI status changes when authorized changes and releases are implemented;
- recording of baselines of CIs and CI packages, to which to revert with known consequences - for example, if an implemented change fails.

Configuration auditing

Automating configuration audits significantly increases the efficiency and effectiveness of the audits. Audit tools can determine exactly what software is installed and identify most critical aspects of hardware configuration. This means a greater coverage of audited CIs with the resources available, and staff can focus on handling the exceptions rather than doing the audits.

Note: automated audits can often only detect certain aspects of a configuration, and sometimes this concerns data that are added manually to a CI. Automated tools also cannot determine whether a CI should have been found or not - they can only detect that a CI is there. This means that the collected data are not guaranteed to be truly reflecting the real status of a CI, let alone the official status. Automated data collection can therefore only *support* the audit of the infrastructure, it can never *replace* it.

Enterprise system and tools

Keeping the above in mind, automated tools allow:
- the collection of up-to-date information for management decisions;
- faster ability to analyze and present management information to underpin decision making;
- centralization of key functions;
- automation of core IT Service Management functions;
- integration of IT Service Management data;
- analysis of raw data and trend identification;
- identification of preventive measures to be implemented;
- assistance with service improvement plans;
- management of growth;
- insight into cost of delivering IT services;
- reduction of risk and uncertainty (better knowledge of services);
- timely and efficient handling of threats to the IT infrastructure.

Sample IT Service Management tool compatibility criteria for Change Management & Configuration Management:
- change request records can be created, changed and deleted;
- each change request record has a unique ID;
- time and date will be automatically recorded in the change request record;
- change request records are separated from incident and problem records;
- change request records can be classified according to priority and category;
- change request records contain status information;
- change request records can be linked to configuration items;
- assessment information can be recorded against the change request;
- change requests can be authorized or rejected;
- communication of authorization or rejection is automated;
- change coordination can be facilitated through the build, test, and implementation phases;
- change request records can be linked to and routed to support employees;
- facilitation with change scheduling;
- change records permit the recording of post implementation assessment and review information;
- changes are monitored and tracked against tolerance breach;

- support for notification and escalation on tolerance breach;
- provides Management information about the process.

Other tools

Efficient management and delivery of IT systems and services requires a mature approach and application of a proven IT Service Management framework. The most widely accepted such framework available today is ITIL®. Equally important is the task of ensuring that IT organizations are equipped with the right tools. Real IT Service Management benefits are realized through process data integration. This section will address the following questions:

- What are the technological functionality requirements for underpinning IT Service Management processes?
- How can automation of data integration assist organizations in achieving their organizational objectives?

The sophistication, complexity, and integration of functional tool requirements should be driven by defined IT processes. Too often, organizations experiencing difficulty in delivering IT services look to technology as a silver bullet to cure their pain. A large amount of money is spent on hardware and software solutions, which may or may not be a proper fit for the organization. This results in the tools being misused, incorrectly configured, or underutilized due to a lack of defined processes.

Software and hardware tools are important and indispensable assets in IT dependent organizations. The starting point should always be to first look at the way in which the IT processes work. As more organizations realize this fact, they are looking to ITIL to provide an industry best practice model for determining tool selection criteria.

Why the need for tools?
- more sophisticated customer demands;
- increased core business dependence on IT services;
- IT skills shortage and the need to capture and reuse knowledge;
- IT budget constraints - the need to cost justify IT spending and relate to business benefits;
- improved customer service requirements;
- increased security considerations and requirements;
- integration of multi-vendor environments;
- increasing complexity of IT infrastructure;
- emergence of 'recognized' and 'adopted' international standards;
- increased scope and frequency of IT changes;
- increased demands on IT to provide return on investment;
- increased requirements for sharing data between IT Service Management processes.

There are many support tools that can assist Change Management, Configuration Management and Release Management. These may come in a variety of combinations and include:
- document management systems;
- requirements analysis and design tools, systems architecture and CASE tools;
- database management audit tools to track physical databases;
- distribution and installation tools;

- comparison tools;
- build and release tools;
- installation and de-installation tools;
- compression tools;
- listing and configuration baseline tools;
- audit tools;
- detection and recovery tools;
- reporting tools;
- knowledge management tools.

5.7   Configuration Management tips & templates

What follows is a set of practical suggestions to make Configuration Management easier to implement and control:

- Automate software and hardware auditing, to support regular reviews.
- Enforce strict record-keeping and controls on software-protection devices ('dongles') because they are valuable assets and often irreplaceable. Keep spares in case of emergencies.
- Reduce the number of officially supported platforms within an organization.
- Minimize the number of variants (both hardware and software) that exist in the live environment (see paragraph 5.7.5 for more details on variants). This makes support much easier and more reliable. Keep an "officially approved hardware and software list".
- Provide mechanisms for users to determine versions of software installed and hardware information. In other words, set up a 'Help About' function for a workstation as whole, not just individual applications.
- Check critical files for their integrity at start-up, for example using checksums.
- Avoid continuing to pay maintenance on hardware or software that has been made redundant by a subsequent roll-out. In addition, it may be possible to use the audit services of Configuration Management to check that no illegal copies of software are installed. This can be performed both as part of a distribution and via ad-hoc audits. This requires a fair degree of automation to do effectively.
- Enforce strict desktop control via policies within the operating system to reduce the chance of the end users changing the target platforms. Note that software developers typically need more open access, or even two workstations, to do their work.

To support the Configuration Management process, the following techniques and templates are included in more detail:
1. Configuration Management roles;
2. CMDB structures and relationships between tables;
3. CI naming and coding conventions;
4. labeling policy;
5. version management conventions.

5.7.1   Configuration Management roles

Configuration Manager responsibilities
Organizing the Configuration Management process as part of the Release & Control processes:
- Develop and implement the organisation's Configuration Management policy, standards, plans and scope.
- Organize the exchange of appropriate information to and from other IT Service Management processes, users and suppliers.
- Maintain the baselines of configurations and status information of Configuration Items.

Managing the Configuration Management process as part of the Release & Control processes:
- Arrange recruitment and training of staff.
- Plan and execute population of the CMDB.
- Manage and maintain a trustworthy CMDB.
- Provide accurate information mechnaisms to support other processes.

Optimizing the Configuration Management process as part of the Release & Control processes:
- Monitor and optimize the Configuration Management process.
- Propose improvements, based on results of monitoring and reviews.
- Plan and conduct configuration audits and reviews.

Configuration Librarian responsibilities
The major tasks of this role are to:
- Control the receipt, identification, storage, and withdrawal of all supported CIs.
- Provide information on the status of CIs.
- Number, record, store and distribute Configuration Management issues.

Specific responsibilities are to:
- Assist in the identification of products and CIs.
- Maintain current status information on CIs.
- Archive superseded CI copies.
- Produce configuration status accounting reports.
- Assist in conducting configuration audits.

The organization should allocate the task to manage the physical components in the DSL and the DHS. This task is often combined with the other tasks of the Configuration Librarian. The Configuration Librarian then is the custodian and guardian of all master copies of software and documentation CIs registered with Configuration Management. Consequently the following tasks are added to this profile:
- Create libraries or other storage areas to hold CIs.
- Hold the master copies in DSL and DHS.

5.7.2   CMDB structures and relationships between tables

Many organizations have, as an inventory system, a set of tables, spreadsheets or documented lists. Often, those documents are dispersed in the organization and sometimes the information contained in them is duplicated or inaccurate.

This set of information, although searchable, does not make it easy for technical staff or management to quickly find the information sought because of the wide variety of location and file formats. Moreover, if information about one component of the infrastructure is found, it is virtually impossible to understand how it fits and interrelates with the rest of the infrastructure.

The goal of the CMDB is to offer an accurate image of the real IT infrastructure and make it accessible from a central access point. From the image, it must be easy to identify a component and identify the interrelationships.

In order to achieve this goal the CMDB will, most likely, take the form of a relational database. This database will be composed of many tables containing information about specific types of components or Configuration Items (CIs).

Tables and specific CIs will be connected through relationships to express the fact that there is a relationship between them, creating some kind of web structure. These relationships need to help IT staff understand how certain CIs affect others or how a CI depends upon other CIs. The number of relationships should not be limited as long as they are pertinent to the IT organization.

The traditional content of the CMDB tables identifies servers, personal computers (PCs), software versions, applications, network components and lists of relevance to the way IT services are delivered and supported.

More precisely, there often are tables for the following components: applications servers, file & print servers, certain key components such as hard disks, applications, modules, databases, commercial software, licenses, routers, switches. There should also be tables listing documents such as application and software user guides, training material, configuration and installation procedures, functional and technical specifications, and system architecture documents. Each of these tables will have its own list of attributes.

The more granular the table structure is, the more flexibility it offers to the IT staff to adapt the infrastructure image, but on the other hand it requires more effort to define and maintain the image. The level of detail (or level of granularity) is dictated by the way an IT organization manages its infrastructure components and how it builds releases units. Figure 5.5 shows an example of what can be registered in a CMDB.

Although the CMDB needs to be accessible from a central point, this does not mean that the CMDB is completely centralized in a unique table or even in a unique system. Tables outside the Service Management system could be integrated with the 'central' image as long as duplication of information is avoided and relationships are defined to link to 'outside' tables and records. For performance purpose, sometimes part of a table will be replicated in another system in order to make data easily available. When the CMDB structure is set up this way (see Figure 5.6 for an example), it is important to clearly establish which system contains the official data and which one is simply a replication (for consultation only).

It should be noted that there are as many different CMDB structures as there are organizational contexts. However, very often the information required from one IT organization to another will be similar. The key is to understand how the information is being used by the different groups and to propose a structure which will allow easy access to the right information and allow easy maintenance of that information.

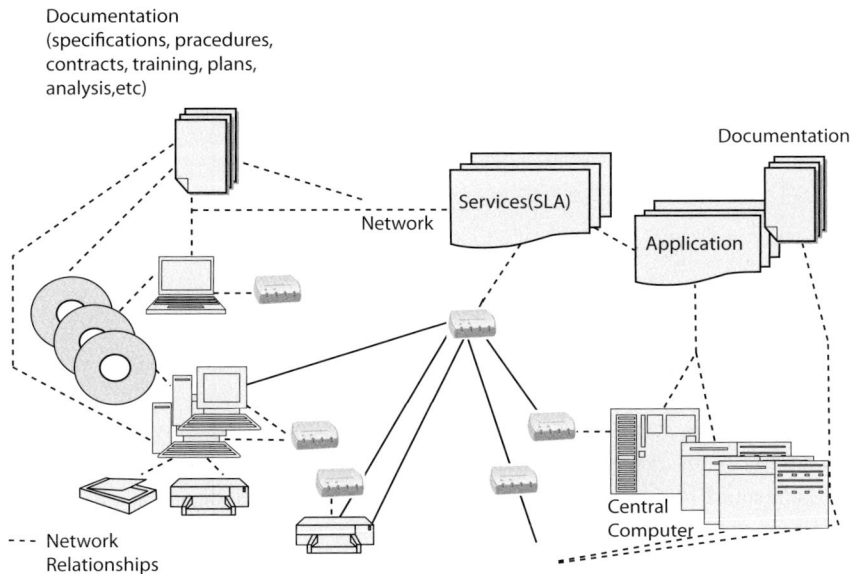

Figure 5.5   Configuration items in a CMDB

5.7.3 CI naming and coding conventions

Configuration Management best practice dictates that a standard naming convention should be established for new and existing CIs within the IT infrastructure. This policy and procedure will need to interface with the acquisition and procurement practices being employed within the IT organization.

The defined naming convention should be unique and take into account existing corporate or supplier naming & numbering structures. It is recommended that names should be kept short and as meaningful as possible. A naming convention should provide insight into location, type, ownership, et cetera and serve as a unique identifier for the CI to be recorded and referenced in the CMDB.

Why is a structured file naming convention needed?

CIs added to the IT infrastructure become part of a complex variety of technical systems co-existing within the organization. It is important that the location, purpose and relationship of the new CI be identified and recorded according to a well thought out naming and labeling policy. A label is needed that identifies the 'who, what, when and how' about each CI. A structured name is an organized approach to building such a label.

Note that it is beneficial to err on the side of being too long rather than too short. It is better to include all relevant elements in a CI naming convention than to use abbreviations that are hard to interpret for the uninitiated.

The adoption of naming conventions makes the management and control of hardware, software, network and documentation entities much easier and identification much simpler, especially for Incident and Change Management. The naming conventions must be standardized and applied

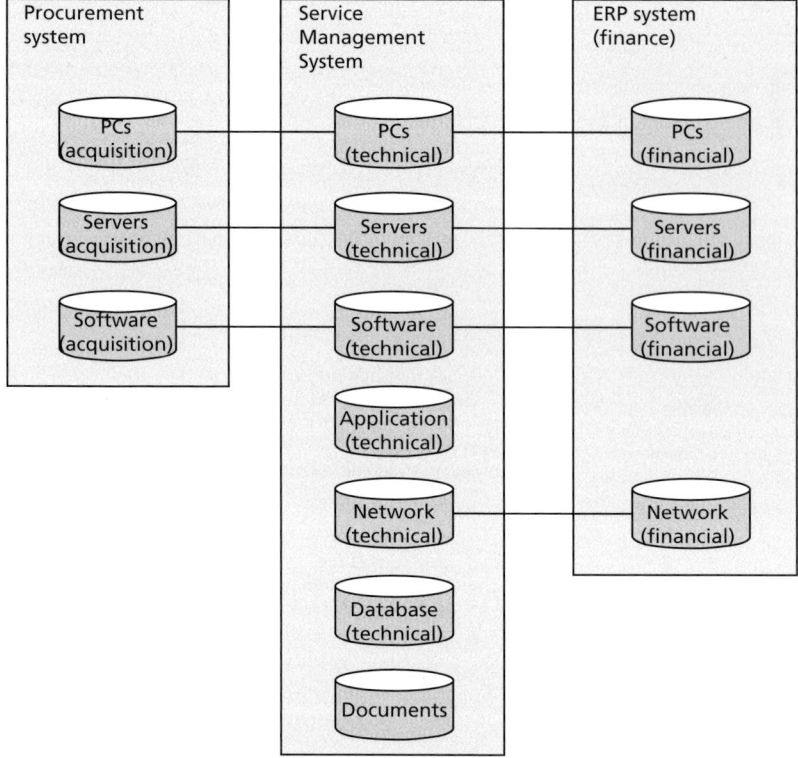

Figure 5.6   An example of a distributed CMDB structure

across all IT departments. The following proposed naming conventions take into account existing corporate and vendor naming & numbering structures.

Applying one and the same naming convention for all CIs promotes clarity and efficiency. However, the number of hardware and network CIs will be much higher compared to software and documentation CIs. For this reason, three naming conventions are described below.

Naming convention for hardware and network devices
The central idea behind the proposed primary naming convention for hardware equipment and network devices has been a simple yet meaningful design that allows for a large number of unique names.

Naming convention for software
The naming convention for software typically follows the naming practice of the development or external vendor organization with an additional recommendation: the naming of software must include the version number.

In case new software is introduced into the IT infrastructure, a request for naming must be submitted to the Configuration Manager to issue a unique name. For this purpose Configuration Management keeps a list of issued software names to secure the unique naming of software.

Naming convention for documentation
The naming convention for documentation typically follows the naming practice similar to the software naming convention.

In case new documentation is introduced into the IT infrastructure, a request for naming must be submitted to the Configuration Manager to issue a unique name. For this purpose Configuration Management keeps a list of issued documentation names to secure the unique naming of documentation.

5.7.4 Labeling policy
The previous section focused on the identification and the naming of CI records in the CMDB. Labeling the actual assets completes the identification of CIs by linking them with records in the CMDB.

Physical labeling
Each physical CI, whether it is hardware equipment, network device or original document, must be labeled with a visible tag indicating the configuration identifier (ID code). Tag format and design must be standardized and applied across all IT departments.

Measures are required to ensure that:
• identifiers printed on tags are unique;
• tags are difficult to remove or leave marks when removed;
• tags self-destruct upon removal, thereby preventing using it again;
• tags are attached at a fixed, visible and accessible spot, depending on the CI type.

Recognizable tags on office equipment will greatly enhance identification by specialists as well as end users. For example, when the end user reports an incident, they can easily find the ID code and communicate this code to the Service Desk. Adding a barcode to the tag or using RFID tags can greatly improve the efficiency and reliability of physical audits.
All media containing software must be clearly labeled with the ID code of each of the software items contained on the media (as well as the ID code of the medium itself).
Originals of documentation are never issued, but are retained in the library. The cover page must be clearly labeled with the ID code of the document. Read-only softcopies of original documents are stored on a central file server and administered by the Configuration Librarian.

Soft coding
Soft coding is the practice of electronic or digital labeling of hardware and network devices. Soft coding enables Configuration Management to execute automated, remote inventories and reviews of physical assets with the use of remote management tools. For this purpose, physical CIs must be soft coded, where possible. The soft code must correspond exactly with the physical tag on the CI. This requires the implementation of a standardized method of entering soft codes

on devices across all IT departments. This includes programming inventory scripts and installing remote agents that collect soft coded information.

5.7.5   Version management conventions

Naming convention need to be established for all CIs. Each CI must be uniquely identifiable by means of the CI's name, copy/serial number and version. The details about the copy/serial number and version are stored in the CMDB, but it does not need be part of the unique identifier.

The Release & Control processes must put in place effective and efficient controls to ensure that updated versions of CIs (hardware, software and documentation) are built correctly and distributed to the appropriate target environments. Versions of software, hardware and documentation that were the result of the Build and Release processes should be recorded and reported on. More than one version of the same CI can co-exist at the same time.

When quality-control checks are successful, the software is authorized for acceptance and copied into the DSL. Care should be taken to ensure that software is not corrupted or changed during the copying or distribution processes. Additionally, hardware baselines will be stored in the DHS and original documents stored in the document library. The appropriate CMDB records will be updated or created.

Versions vs. Variants

Although the same CI cannot be used in more than one location in an IT infrastructure, it is quite possible to use a slightly different version of what could otherwise be regarded as the same CI. This slightly different version would have a different version number, and such CIs are called 'variants'.

A simple analogy using the automotive industry can be used to illustrate this: a car manufacturer often offers variants of the same car model; coupe, sedan and hatchback for example. All the parts are the same except for a few differences. Maintenance is easier, standardization of interchangeable parts makes repairs easier and cheaper.

In IT variants are used all the time. Printer manufacturers offer models that have two, three or four paper trays. Software offered in many languages uses the variant approach. It is the same software but with some differences to handle the various languages and characters. English will be left to right, Arabic, right to left for example.

There is normally a trade-off involved. The use of variants can result in fewer CIs to manage and may make it easier to identify items for commonality of treatment, be this in error handling or for the implementation of changes. The use of variants will, however, introduce extra complexity to the Configuration Management system, and/or other systems such as Problem Management that rely on it.

General guidance is thus: if a CI can be regarded as slightly different from another related CI, and problems affecting one are likely to affect the other, or changes made to the one will probably have to be made to the other, then use of a variant should be considered; otherwise, a different CI should be used.

There are normally dependencies between a particular version of software and the hardware required for it to operate. This will drive the packaging of software and hardware together to form a new release of the service, along with other functional requirements. For example, a new version of an application software system may require an upgrade to the operating system and one or other of these two changes could require a hardware change, e.g. a faster processor or more memory.

Versions should be uniquely identified according to a scheme defined in the Release Policy. The version identification should include a reference to the CI that it represents and a version number that will often have two or three parts. For example:

- CI Name, Major #, Minor #, Emergency Fix #.
- Payroll_System 1.0 - indicates that this is the first major version of the payroll system, that there has not been any minor or emergency releases yet.
- Payroll_System 1.1.2 - indicates that this is the first major version of the payroll system, that there has been one minor release and two emergency releases since the minor.
- Payroll_System 2.2.1 - indicates that is the second major version of the payroll system, that there have been two minor and one emergency release since the minor.

For further details on release numbering and software version, please refer to the Release Management chapter.

5.8   Knowledge test questions

Question 1

Which of the following elements does not belong in the CMDB?

A.   The technical information about the network switches
B.   The default profiles (access rights) of the systems users
C.   The program code of an ERP module
D.   The associations between software and the PCs on which it is installed

Question 3

The initial planning of Configuration Management includes activities such as:

1.   Gaining agreement on the purpose, objectives, scope, priority and approach for Configuration Management
2.   Analyzing existing Configuration Management systems, data and processes
3.   Developing a high level Configuration Plan
4.   Planning for and obtaining financing for a Configuration Management tool and extra resources
5.   Agreeing on the corporate policy and processes, and defining what can be tailored during roll-out

What other activity is part of that phase?

A.   Do an initial discovery of all CI
B.   Assign a person to be responsible for Configuration Management
C.   Do the project plan
D.   Determine which indicators will be used for process control

Question 3
Different types of relationships with a CI can be found in the CMDB. Which of the following is
not an example of a relationship that can be found in the CMDB?
A.   A relationship between an application and the server it is hosted on
B.   A relationship between a PC and an incident record for that PC
C.   A relationship between the incident record for a PC and the solution which was used to
     correct the incident
D.   A relationship between a Sever and an RFC to upgrade its operating system

Question 4
During the CI control portion of the process, which of the following activities should be taking
place?
1.   Record new CIs created by the development teams
2.   Update existing CIs (attributes, relationships, status etc.) following changes to them
3.   Remove from the CMDB, CIs which were removed from the infrastructure
4.   Back-up and Archive CMDB data
5.   Produce reports on the number of CI in the CMDB and modifications to them
6.   Execute periodic verification between the CMDB content and the actual elements in the
     infrastructure
7.   Protecting integrity of configurations
8.   Update the CMDB after verifying the existence of physical items

A.   1,2,3,4,5,6
B.   1,2,3,7,8
C.   6,8
D.   1,2,3,5,7

5.9   Practical assignments

5.9.1   Exercise 1: 'Managing'
Working in appropriately divided groups, brainstorm the following:
•   benefits, challenges & costs;
•   training requirements; and
•   policy issues

… of implementing the **Configuration Management** process

5.9.2   Exercise 2: 'Organizing'
1.   Review the following Configuration Management process flow diagram.
2.   Present arguments whether it is a workable model for managing the day-to-day activities of
     the Configuration Management process.
3.   You may modify the process flow to ensure that all activities of the process are covered.
4.   Present any recommendations for improvement of the process, if any.

The diagram in figure 5.7 illustrates a simple sample process flow (not necessarily ITIL compatible)
for developing and maintaining the CMDB. Adding/updating a CI process flow:

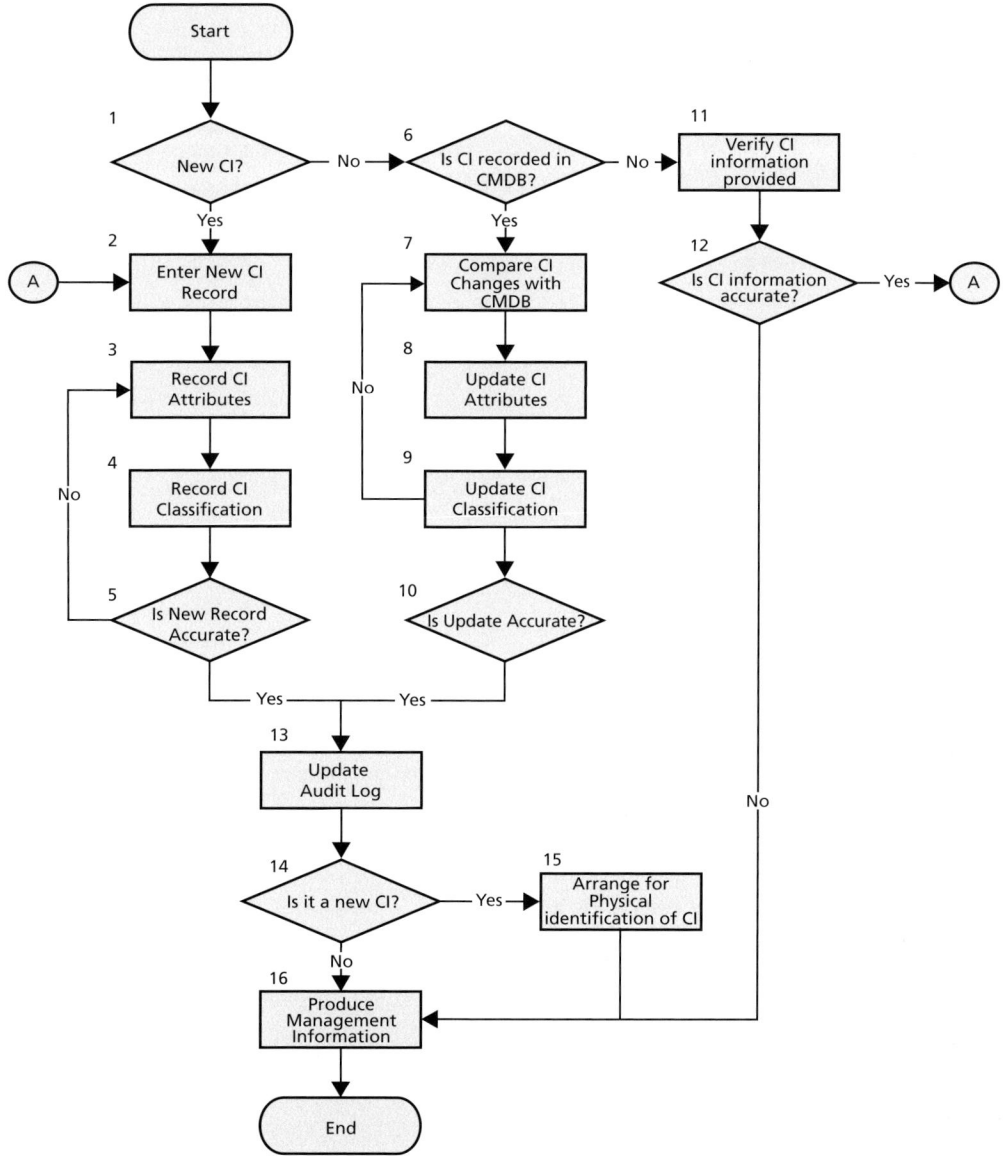

Figure 5.7   CI Process Flow

5.9.3 Exercise 3: 'Optimizing'

A Key Performance Indicator is used to demonstrate one or more of the following qualifiers:

- Value
- Quality
- Performance
- Compliance

Identify for the Configuration Management process, which KPIs are used to demonstrate:
- Value
- Quality
- Performance
- Compliance

Configuration Management	Value	Quality	Performance	Compliance
Control of IT Assets				
Percentage reduction in number of Configuration Item (CI) attribute errors found in Configuration Management Database (CMDB)				
Percentage increase in the number of CIs successfully audited				
Percentage improvements in the speed and accuracy of audit				
Support the delivery of quality IT services				
Percentage reduction in service errors attributable to wrong CI information				
Improved speed of component repair and recovery				
Improved customer satisfaction with services and terminal equipment				
Economic Service Provision				
Reduction in the number of 'missing or duplicated' CIs				
Greater percentage of maintenance costs and license fees within budget				
Percentage reduction in software costs (development, licenses) due to better control				
Percentage reduction in hardware costs due to better control of spares inventory and supplies				
Percentage improvement in average cost of maintaining CIs in CMDB				
Support, Integration and Interfacing to all other ITSM Processes				
Reduced percentage of change failures as a result of inaccurate configuration data				
Improved incident resolution time due to the availability of complete and accurate configuration data				
More accurate results from Risk Analysis audits due to available and accurate asset information				

Table 5.2   KPIs for Configuration Management process

6   Release Management

6.1   Introduction

6.1.1   High level overview

Figure 6.1 shows an overview of the position of Release Management in between other processes.

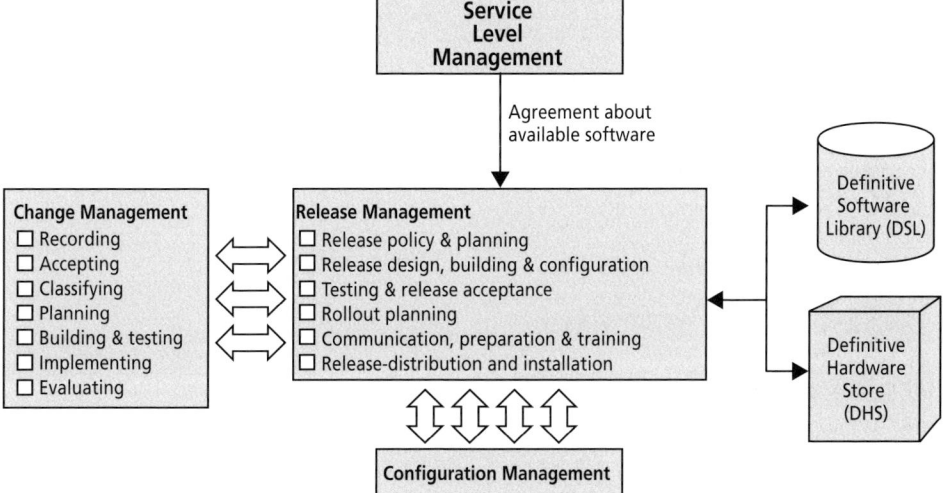

Figure 6.1   The position of Release Management (Source: itSMF)

Figure 6.2 shows the main activities of Release Management. The diagram should not be read as a flow chart, we should distinguish between:
• Time based/periodic activities, such as Release Policy design and maintenance.
• Event based activities that are triggered by approved changes: i.e. the others.

6.1.2   Goal

The goal of Release Management is to take a holistic view of a change to an IT service and ensure that all aspects of a release, both technical and non-technical, are considered together.

6.1.3   Scope

Release Management works closely together with Change and Configuration Management. Changes are first reviewed and approved by Change Management, then coordinated with Release Management for bundling into releases and distributing the release to the target system or user(s). Release also liaises with Configuration Management to ensure all Configuration Items are updated to reflect the release. Key activities include:
• planning and overseeing the successful roll-out of new and changed software and associated hardware and documentation;

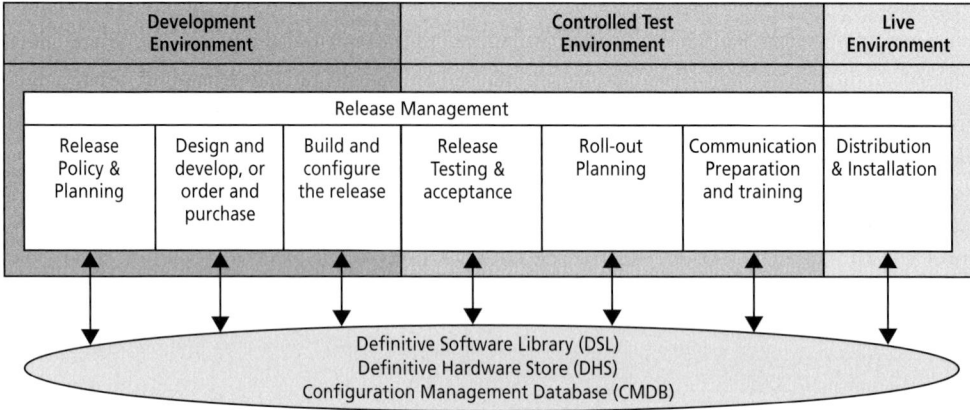

Figure 6.2   Release Management activities

- liaison with Change Management to agree the exact content and roll-out plan for the release;
- ensuring that all items being rolled out or changed are secure and traceable via the CMDB;
- managing customer and user expectations of releases and roll-outs.

6.1.4   Basic Concepts – Terminology

Release, release unit, release types and Release Policy

Release	A collection of authorized changes to an IT service.
Release unit	The portion of the IT infrastructure that is normally released together.
Release identification	Unique release identifying scheme which is defined in the Release Policy. Examples: • Major Release: Billing system V1, V2 … • Minor Release: Billing System V1.1, V1.2 ,… • Emergency Fix release: Billing System V1.1.1, V1.1.2 …
Types of release	• *Delta* - Also known as partial release; only includes CIs within the release unit that have actually changed. • *Full* - Release of a completely new version of an application; e.g. Windows XP is replaced by Vista. All components of the release unit are purchased/built, tested and distributed together. • *Package* - Combination of several Delta release units and/or Full releases to reduce the frequency of roll-outs or to build, test and roll-out related releases which can influence each other.
Categories of release	• *Major Release* - A large planned upgrade of the IT service, with major new functionality. • *Minor Release* - A smaller update between Major Releases, with small improvements or corrections. • *Emergency Fix* - Urgent release, for example to take away a fault in the infrastructure that causes multiple or major incidents. An Emergency Fix cannot wait until the next Minor or Major Release.

Table 6.1   Release definitions

The **Release Policy** defines the roles and responsibilities for Release Management. The policy covers release numbering, frequency and the level in the IT infrastructure that will be controlled by definable releases. There may be one policy, addressing all aspects of Release Management in an organization or one umbrella policy defining guidelines, with additional documents defining specifics for each system or IT service.

Release Management should comply with the Release Policy of the customer. For example, if the customer wants only four releases of an Information System per year, Release Management as well as Change Management have to comply to this.

Release Management plans releases when Change Management has authorized the changes that make up the release. Based on the types of authorized changes, Release Management will collaborate with Change Management to decide which changes will be released together. Release Management needs to balance the desire to combine changes, which may minimize downtime or allow for changes to be implemented more quickly, while keeping the risk of making too many changes at once, which can reduce the likelihood of success, in check.

DSL, DHS and CMDB
The **Definitive Software Library (DSL)** and **Definitive Hardware Store (DHS)** are both physical storage for components of a release. The DSL that can also be logical (or physical and logical) contains the master copies of all controlled software versions in the organization, including purchased and in-house developed software. It can be centralized or decentralized.
The DHS is a secure storage area for all authorized types of hardware in use. Authorized spare configurations should be located at the same place as the live components. All the components of the DSL and DHS are CIs and are recorded and tracked via the CMDB.

Key decisions for establishing the DSL include deciding what media format will be used, naming conventions for releases, security, the scope of contents, retention period and audit procedures. The DSL should be routinely backed up, with copies stored off-site to support the IT Service Continuity recovery plans (see the Appendices chapter for a DSL design sample).

Deciding the contents of the DHS will often involve interaction with other Service Management processes. Availability Management will recommend which CIs be stored on site in order to reduce the incident repair and recovery times to ensure attainment of availability related Service Level Agreements. Problem Management may also make recommendations as a result of incident and problem analysis.

Build Management, Testing, Roll-out and Back-out Plans
The software, hardware and documentation that comprise a new release should be assembled in a controlled manner to ensure a reproducible process. When possible, automation should be used to reduce the likelihood of human error during the actual roll-out. For custom applications, Build Management becomes the responsibility of Release Management from the controlled test environment onwards.

Developers do not have access to the live environment. They deliver their input to Release Management, who handle the new or revised software and hardware via the DSL to the test environment.

New versions should undergo stringent testing and user acceptance before release. This involves replicating the live environment as closely as possible. Release Management provides this environment. Testing should include the replication of the roll-out procedures to ensure a smooth roll-out. Back-out procedures need to be defined and tested to ensure a smooth recovery, in case the roll-out of the release would fail. Decision criteria should also be clearly defined and agreed upon during planning, for triggering the back-out procedures. For example, if a release is not completed within a certain timeframe, the back-out plan will be initialized.

Release Management should set up a Quality Assurance environment to test new releases. Quality Assurance has to be built on same hardware as the live environment to be able to:
• test performance;
• test software functionality on same versions of operating system software;
• set up to test back-out capacities.

6.1.5   Roles and Responsibilities of Release Management

The following roles may be considered. A detailed description of these roles can be found in the sample 'Release Management Roles' in the 'Tips & Templates' section. An exhaustive description of the different release roles can be found as an appendix.
• **Release Management Process Owner:**
  – takes ownership over the process to establish accountability;
  – ensures there is a balance between the key components of a good Service Management environment: People, Technology/Tool, Process and Steering.
• **Release Manager:**
  – establishes accountability for the day-to-day operation of the process;
  – creates a responsible monitoring function.
• **Release Manager Assistant:**
  – assists the Release Manager in day-to-day operation of the process;
  – shares the workload of Release Manager;
  – deputizes for the Release Manager, when and if required, providing greater accessibility to the Release Management process.
• **Release Coordinator:**
  – establishes a coordination function within the department, project team or section in which they are working;
  – executes activities in adherence to the applicable procedures and instructions of the Process.
• **Definitive Software Librarian:**
  – establishes an administrative function for the day-to-day management of the Definitive Software Library.

6.2 Topics & theory 'Manage'

The key activities for Release Management in the Release & Control processes are:
- define the Release Policy;
- plan the release process;
- set up the DSL and DHS.

In ITIL, releases are positioned as being changes of a specific kind: where new versions of infrastructure are deployed. As a result, Change Management governs Release Management. However, in a wider perspective, it seems reasonable to have Change Management follow Release Management, the other way around. It is the customer who initially agrees a Release Policy with the IT service provider, and confirms this in the SLA. The Release Policy then is the leading document, and changes should be assessed against the agreed Release Policy. The planning of changes that involve new versions would then be subject to the Release Policy. Once a change involving a new version is accepted, is will trigger the Release Management process. This will put the release planning in the lead, and still have releases under the control of Change Management.

For this chapter, we will follow the definitions and explanations of the ITIL Service Support book.

6.2.1 Release Policy

The role of the Release Policy is to define the main roles and responsibilities of Release Management, especially in relationship to Change and Configuration Management. Change Management, for example, will delegate authority to Release Management in case of standard releases.

In relationship to Configuration Management it must be clear who holds what responsibility for administering the DSL, DHS, versions and licenses.

Suggested items to include in the Release Policy are:
- release numbering;
- frequency;
- definition of releases; i.e. Minor, Major and Emergency Fix;
- level of automation and tool use, i.e. SMS;
- terms and definitions to include in the Release Policy;
- release unit;
- release identification;
- types of releases:
  - Delta Release;
  - Package Release;
  - Full Release.

The Release Manager is responsible for the population of the Definitive Software Library (DSL) and for the communication of changes to Configuration Management. In the DSL the delivered versions from the builders are identified by a unique version number. The format of this version number depends on the type of release.

A possible format is:

[Release number – [Release name] [Software version] ([Release version])

- **Release number** - each release gets the next higher number.
- **Release name** - the name of the bundled release.
- **Software version** - the version as gotten from the original software builder, could be the supplier.
- **Release version** - the version as this is concluded by the CAB. Syntax: [X.Y.Z]: X is added with 1 if it is a new Major Release. Y is added with 1 if it is a Minor Release, Z is added with 1 if it is an Emergency Fix.

The information about the versions is kept in the CMDB as metadata.

6.2.2 Plan the release process

Several issues should be addressed during Release Planning. In the first place there should be consensus between the main stakeholders; i.e. Functional or Information Management, Applications Management and the Operations groups.

The following areas may be of relevance depending on the specific organizational context:

- agreement on the timescale of specific releases;
- agreement on the order of release when dealing with geographically dispersed organizations; the same may be relevant when different culture or language aspects play a role; site surveys may be necessary;
- initial Release Schedule as input for the later roll-out planning;
- available local and centralized resources;
- involvement of third parties;
- quality criteria from the perspective of the different stakeholders;
- involvement of staff, both IT and customer, in the different test stages.

In Table 6.2 the main Inputs and Outputs of Release Planning are listed.

INPUTS:		OUTPUTS:
Authorized RFCs / CAB minutes		
Project Plans		
Forward Schedule of Change and Release		Detailed Release Plan
Maintenance Calendar		CAB recommendations
Project deliverables	➡	Roll-out planning
Summary of business case		Test plans
Release Policy constraints		Acceptance criteria
Case tools and templates		Resource planning

Table 6.2 Input and Output of Release Planning

The following activities could be part of the Release Planning procedure:
- Determine the scope of the release:
  - Will a third party deliver a tested release, and if so what does this mean for licensing and support?
  - Do we need to lease extra hardware?
  - What type is it (i.e. Emergency Fix, delta, full or package)?
- Prioritize the release:
  - Here we will need to cross reference with the Release Policy.
- Determine the release (project) team composition:
- Are other activities needed:
  - Training, specific site related logistics or communications.
- Final check with the Release Policy, Forward Schedule of Change (FSC) and Maintenance Calendar:
  - If the requirements change there may be referral back to the Change Advisory Board for re-evaluation and approval.

6.2.3 Setting up the DSL and DHS
Procedures should be put in place defining all design criteria, key relationships and all other requirements for the DSL and DHS. The following stakeholders should be consulted and involved at this stage:
- Change Manager and Configuration Manager
- Applications support group
- Information Management group
- Development project organization

Furthermore, procedures and work instructions for everyday use of the DSL and DHS should be drafted at this stage. Combined, these can form the DSL and DHS handbook.
The following example shows the table of contents of such a document for the DSL. Like the Release Policy, this document may be part of the Configuration & Change Management plan.

Other detail issues for the CMDB as well as the DSL can be:
- setup database items including:
  - system information
  - system type
  - hardware driver version and patches
  - operating software versions and patches
  - application software versions and patches, application packages versions, and Emergency Fixes
- for each item :
  - name
  - version
  - date of implementation
  - name of implementer
  - name of tester
  - change request number
  - name of developer.

Table of Contents	
1	Introduction
1.1	Purpose of this document
1.2	Document management
1.3	Purpose of the DSL
1.4	Scope of the DSL
1.5	Starting-up phase and development of the DSL in the future
1.6	Relationships with other IT Processes
1.6.1	Change Management
1.6.2	Configuration Management
1.7	Standardisation of software versions
1.8	Making software online available
2	Policies and requirements for the DSL
2.1	Policy for storing software in DSL
2.2	Requirements to the physical DSL
2.3	Naming and numbering convention for software
2.4	Authorization
3	Procedures and work instructions
3.1	Receiving and storing
3.2	Lending out
3.3	Return after lending out
3.4	Removal of software from DSL
3.5	Detection and retrieval of not-returned software
3.6	Reporting

Table 6.3   Sample table of contents for a DSL handbook

6.3   Topics & theory 'Organize'

6.3.1   Release planning operations

Define the scope of the release
The Release Manager will coordinate the discussion to determine the scope of the release. The change may be handled as a single release or it may be combined with other RFCs for a Package Release. Release Management will consider the urgency of the change and the impact of this change on the existing Release Schedule. All activities will be according to the Release Policy.

Identify the Release Team
The Release Manager will identify the appropriate virtual team for the release. Team members may have already been identified in the RFC, but the Release Manager will ensure all appropriate disciplines are represented, considering for example, the technology, operations, support, security, testing and the business. The Release Manager will initiate the start-up of the team to ensure roles, responsibilities and expectations are established.

> **Resourcing Release Management**
> Since the Release Team is often a cross-functional team it is important that expectations for
> participation, roles and responsibilities are defined when Release Management is established
> in the organization. Establishing Operational Level Agreements (OLAs) between functional
> groups participating in the Release, Change and Configuration Management process is an
> effective means for facilitating this discussion and coming to agreement on how resources will
> be allocated and what response times are needed for release activities (see Appendices chapter
> for an OLA template).

Establish Release Criteria

Specific criteria should be identified for the release to pass from each stage of the process (see
Figure 2). If any exceptions are identified, a waiver should be signed by the appropriate release,
change and business contacts to ensure agreement and justification for the exception.

At the release planning and development stage, specific requirements and/or templates should be
identified for the required components, including:
• release build requirements;
• release procedures;
• hardware and software procurement requirements;
• test plan, including required test environment and acceptance criteria;
• back-out plan;
• end user documentation.

Only once all required components are developed and documented will the release pass to the
testing stage.
For the testing phase, specific acceptance criteria need to be defined in order for the release to
pass the testing phase and move to roll-out. The acceptance criteria should include:
• successful testing of release procedures;
• successful deployment of the release to the destination using the packaged release files and
  identified hardware;
• successful end user acceptance of the deployed release and end user documentation;
• successful back-out of release in case of failed release and restoration of the user environment
  to the prior working release.

Once the testing meets the acceptance criteria, the release can pass to the roll-out stage. If the
acceptance criteria cannot be met, the release will pass back to the design and build phase for
re-work.

Schedule the Release

The Release Schedule will depend upon the categorization of the change and the schedule for
the plan, build and test phases of the release process. The Release Policy may hold detailed
agreements on specific releases. All releases should then be scheduled against the release policy.
Urgent changes are likely to result in urgent releases. Standard changes, if the risk of business
disruption is minimal, may be released during normal work hours; others will be scheduled for
agreed maintenance or change windows. If no pre-approved windows for change and maintenance
exist, the business may be required to sign-off on the Release Schedule. Normal changes will be

scheduled in conjunction with Change Management, considering resources, other releases and potential impact of the release.

Once the release is scheduled, the schedule should be available to all stakeholders.

6.3.2 Design, Build and Configure

The technical teams will design, build and configure the release and the associated documentation required for the release to pass into the test phase as defined in the release criteria. All activities should be performed in accordance with the Release Policy or exceptions should be noted and signed off.

6.3.3 Acceptance

The testing phase should be performed by separate resources from the development team. The testing team will perform activities identical to the actual roll-out activities to ensure a successful release, using the procedures and success criteria defined in the planning, design and build phases. Issues identified during testing should be documented, including workarounds and resolutions identified. The testing team will work with the build team to address any problems identified and the build team will make the necessary adjustments. If the acceptance criteria cannot be met, the release will pass back to the design and build phase for re-work.

There can be several acceptance environments for several tests: Users Acceptance Test, Production Acceptance Test, Integration Acceptance Test, Control Acceptance Test, Functional Acceptance Test, etcetera. Just as many as are required.

6.3.4 Roll-out Planning

The roll-out planning can now be finalized. The release dates can be confirmed or re-scheduled as needed with agreement from Change Management and the business. Whenever possible, roll-outs should be performed during scheduled maintenance windows, or off-hours to minimize business disruptions or potential disruptions if the release fails. When roll-outs are performed during normal working hours, upfront agreement with the business is critical. Finalization of resources for the roll-out and any training or preparation for the roll-out team should be scheduled. In addition, the roll-out communications and training can be initiated as per the Communication and Training plan.

6.3.5 Communication and Training

The Communication Plan

Effective communications and training are key success factors for many release. The planning for communications and training should begin early in the release planning. Often these activities may involve the use of internal communication or training groups, or external vendors/partners.

The communication planning efforts begin with the identification of the stakeholders for the release. This information should be included in the RFC but may not be complete. The Communication Plan should include:

• identification of all stakeholder groups; identify who will be responsible, accountable, who we will need to influence or consult.
• the message for each stakeholder group;
• 'WIIFM', the 'what's in it for me', for each stakeholder group;

- when the message should be delivered; be sure to consider any dependencies, for example, some messages may require management communication prior to staff communication;
- agreement on who will deliver the message;
- the format of the communication – email, voicemail, team meeting, one-on-one meeting, etc.

Communication planning may require identification of communications for each phase of the release such as planning, implementation and post-release. For additional assistance in creating a Communication Plan, see the Communication Plan template in the Appendices chapter.

The Training Plan

Develop a Training Plan to prepare the users and support staff for the release. See the Training Plan template in the CD to assist with this. The Training Plan should address:
- who needs to be trained;
- the goals and objectives of the training;
- what they need to know;
- the format of the training (lecture, hands-on, group or one-on-one, etc.);
- the timing of the training. The timing should coincide as closely as possible with the actual release. Training too early generates few benefits and often results in excessive calls to the Service Desk for assistance;
- CSFs and KPIs for the training;
- follow up and/or re-enforcement tools such as documentation, quick reference guides, FAQs, self-help websites, etc.

Training needs for the support staff may vary. Typical examples include:
- **Service Desk analysts** - release contents, what users will be affected, FAQs and the answers, escalation procedures and knowledgebase search words.
- **Operational Support staff** – release support requirements, including back-ups and monitoring requirements, release dependencies, escalation procedures and knowledgebase search words.
- **Release staff** – release documents, packages and any unique tools or exceptions, the target audience, business impact and post roll-out testing requirements.

The Training Plan template in the 'Tips & templates' section can help you create a Training Plan.

6.3.6 Distribution and installation

The target production environment needs to be prepared for deployment including:
- creating secure back-ups of all changing CIs, including documentation;
- operations and Support staff are aware of and prepared for the new environment;
- ensuring end users are aware of and prepared for the changing environment and processes if applicable.

A Release Readiness Review is conducted to agree on a go/no go decision for the release. If all target production environment preparedness activities are complete, the release testing has resulted in successful completion of all release criteria and the release date has been approved by the business, the release is clearly a go. If any criteria are not met in entirety, the release is a no go, or an exception is approved by Change, Release Management and the Business representatives.

The release is then performed according to the schedule. The roll-out team will confirm successful deployment of the release and when applicable, there may be final acceptance testing by end users. In either case, the Release Team should be in contact with the support groups monitoring for any incidents related to the release.

If the release is not successful, and the criteria for roll-back are met, the back-out plan will be invoked. Once the back-out is complete, testing should take place to ensure the environment is operable.

6.3.7 Organize/manage the DSL and DHS
For each release, the DSL will be referenced to ensure the most current software versions are released into the environment. When new or updated versions of software are to be released, updating the DSL with the new version according to the Release Policy is a critical step for maintaining the DSL. Older versions may be retired according to the scope of the release and the Release Policy.

Updating the DHS will require evaluation of the impact of the release on any existing hardware store. If no new CI types are released, the evaluation is concerned with considering whether the appropriate amount of spare parts are stored at the right locations considering the release. If new CI types are introduced, consideration needs to be given to extending the store to include new authorized spare parts that support the release. The new release may also result in the retirement of existing authorized spare parts, no longer needed in the environment.

6.3.8 License management (DSL) and Inventory Controls
During the planning stages for the release, the impact of the release on purchased licenses should be evaluated. As previous versions of software are retired, corresponding license renewals should be cancelled. If additional licensing is needed, this should be acquired via the procurement process. When new software CIs are introduced into the environment, the accompanying licenses will also need to be acquired through the procurement process.

Inventory controls for both hardware and software should be automated whenever possible via the CMDB and the release tools. Thresholds can be set for licenses and hardware inventory levels such that when a minimum level is reached, the procurement process can be triggered.

6.4 Topics/theory 'Optimize'

6.4.1 Process Control

Performance Assessment
A number of Key Performance Indicators (KPIs) should be defined and monitored to assess the efficiency and effectiveness of the Release Management process. Because the release process has to create a balance in the demands and requirements of the customer's information management,

applications management and the production environment, a balanced scorecard may be used to create a clear picture.

FINANCIAL	CUSTOMER
• Releases built and implemented within budgeted resources • No unused licenses • No unused maintenance or support for which there are underpinning contracts • Human resources allocated to release projects	• Application functionality rolled out in time for business use • Very low or no release, build or roll-out related incidents • Accurate distribution of releases to all remote sites • Compliance with all legal restrictions relating to bought-in software
• Monitoring results of software development maturity; for example using the Software Capability Maturity Model (SW-CMM) • Process review reports including suggested actions for process improvements	• Low number of build failures • Secure and accurate management of the DSL • No evidence of software in the DSL that has not passed all quality criteria • No differences in DSL and DHS content and the administration of the assets in the CMDB
INNOVATION	INTERNAL

Table 6.4   A sample Balanced Scorecard for Release Management

6.4.2 Important documents Release Management
Important documents for Release Management include:
• official software documentation;
• intake documents;
• acceptation intake by CAB (or others);
• release Plan;
• test plan and the test results;
• technical documentation builder;
• functional documentation for the users environment and Serviced Desk;
• form release-acceptation for OK customer (could be by phase);
• roll-out plan;
• changes to CMDB.

6.4.3 Release Management KPI
An example of a KPI for Release Management:
The DSL and CMDB have to describe the same software.

Do this by setting up authorisations and procedures. Check on completeness. Tooling can help. Make a table with the Responsible persons, the Workers, Authorities and Informed persons.

6.5   Relationships
Figure 6.3 depicts the hierarchical relationship between the three Release & Control processes. Release Management is the operational process where all changes and releases are prepared for roll-out.

The other two processes perform the control functions needed to run the process effectively and efficiently. Change Management forms the Planning and Control level, and Configuration Management the administrative level, enabling Change Management to control all change and release roll-outs. For Release Management Configuration Management stores, controls and verifies all CIs and administers the DSL and DHS.

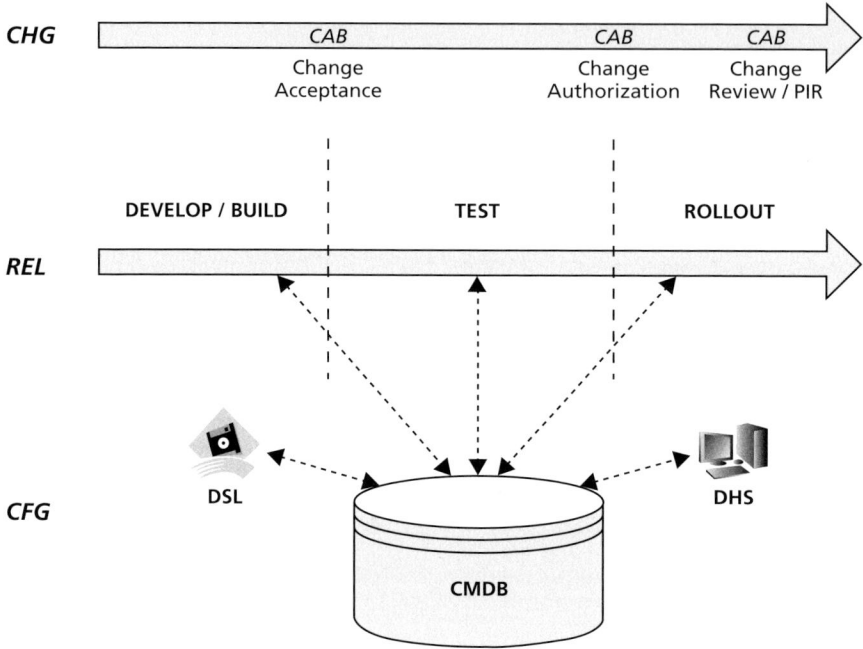

Figure 6.3   The hierarchical relationship between Change- Release- and Configuration Management

6.5.1 Configuration Management

Together with Change Management, Configuration Management forms the controlling mechanism for the IT infrastructure. Therefore, when, as part of Release Build and Testing activities, all new and authorized versions of software are added to the DSL they should be simultaneously included in the CMDB.

Furthermore, when newly purchased hardware is placed in the DHS and later rolled out, the CMDB should be updated. The CMDB should always contain the current status information on all authorized software and hardware and is used to ensure that only authorized and correct components are included in a release.

During the implementation of a release, Release Management will have to rely on several other services from Configuration Management to check if the release was implemented successfully.

Example 1 – Verification and Audit: a Configuration Audit to ensure that the target environment is as expected may be required as part of the release roll-out plan.

Example 2 – License Management: by monitoring and controlling software licenses from purchase to retirement, Configuration Management supports the Release Management process in an administrative as well as a judicial role.

Configuration Management may also manage software license structures, and corporate and multi-licensing schemes.

6.5.2 Change Management

The relationship between Release Management and Change Management cannot be determined without considering the following question:

"Does Release Management deal with both software and hardware changes, new systems and also upgrades?"

In fact the ITIL v2 theory is not always consistent on how it should relate to Change Management in practice. Procedures require 100 per cent clarity on that relationship, otherwise they do not work.

Very often, and especially in the case of the development of legacy applications, the relationship is stressed by the division between the development and live environment. Where the first Release Management stages can be found in the development environment, under control of development project teams, Change Management only comes into the picture when the development project approaches production acceptance testing. When the span of control of Change Management does not cover the whole release project, clear acceptance criteria should be defined for the transition between the two environments. Otherwise the Release Management process cannot function as a whole.

The following best practices were utilized in an implementation at a Telecom Company:
• Implement Change and Release Management at the SAME TIME!
• Have a FULLTIME Process Manager at the beginning of the project!
• Define clearly which environments are controlled by Release Management.

ITIL theory itself defines it in the broadest possible way; describing Release Management to control the development, test and live environment (see Figure 6.4). This, however, is very ambitious, as controlling the development environment demands mature vendor management, Service Level Management and project management.

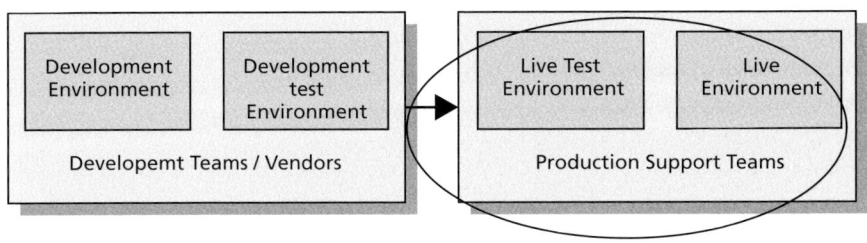

Figure 6.4   Various environments in the life cycle of a release

All authorized changes go to Release Management (thus software, hardware, documentation, new and upgrades). Standard changes and service requests are not included!

6.6   Release management tips & templates

The Release Management samples and templates included in this paragraph are:
- Release roles
- DSL Design
- Release Management procedures
- Release Management Operational Level Agreement
- Communication Plan
- Training Plan

6.6.1   Release management roles and responsibilities

This paragraph provides samples of detailed descriptions of the various roles in the Release Management process. Five roles are described: Release Management Process Owner, Release Manager, Release Manager Assistant, Release Coordinator, Release Management Process Worker, Definitive Software Librarian.

All roles are described in terms of: Objectives, Responsibilities, Activities, Authorities, Competencies and Qualifications, and they can (or should) be represented at any hardware/ software platforms that are involved in Release Management,

Release Management Process Owner
Objective of the role
- take ownership over the process to establish accountability;
- ensure there is a balance between the key components of a good Service Management environment: people, technology/tool, process and steering.

Responsibilities
- ensuring that the Release Management process and governance structure is fit-for-purpose;
- defining the business case for the Release Management process;
- ensuring there is optimal fit between people, process, technology/tool and steering;
- ensuring proper Key Performance Indicators are set;
- ensuring quality reports are produced, distributed, and utilized;
- integrating the process into the line organization;
- taking a 'helicopter view', oversee and ensure integration between Release Management and other processes;
- staying informed about developments of the business;
- staying informed about new ICT and / or ITSM developments.

Activities
- analyze and distribute reports;
- review proposed changes to the Release Management process;
- initiate improvements in the tool, process, steering mechanisms, and people;
- review integration issues between the various processes;

- communicate changes to the Release Management process and governance structure;
- promote the Service Management vision to top-level/ senior management
- function as a point of escalation when required;
- approve and initiate training when required;
- recruit and coach Release Management staff where needed (including the Release Manager);
- attend top-level management meetings to assess the impact of organizational decisions on the Release Management environment;
- schedule and attend meetings according to the Release Management process and governance structure.

Authorities
- has the authority to approve proposed changes to the Release Management process and governance structure;
- cannot enforce the use of the Release Management process, but can escalate any breaches to top-level management;
- can organize training for IT employees and can nominate staff, they cannot oblige any staff to follow training, but can escalate to line management should training be required;
- will negotiate with the relevant process owner if there is a conflict between processes;
- has the authority over the Release Manager and Release Coordinators where process activities are concerned.

Competencies and qualifications
The ideal Release Management Process Owner has the following competencies and qualifications:
- ability to operate with a helicopter view;
- good knowledge about process working;
- ability to coach and mentor process staff;
- general knowledge of IT;
- good knowledge of the organization;
- strong internal network;
- good understanding of the business side;
- ITSM Foundation certificate and moving forward to achieve the ITSM Service Management certificate;
- ability to act as a serious counterpart at Director or General Manager level.

Release Manager
Objective of the role
- establish accountability for the day-to-day operation of the process;
- create a responsible monitoring function.

Responsibilities
- ensure and promote the (correct) use of the Release Management process;
- ensure management and other processes are provided with steering information;
- ensure the Release Management Key Performance Indicators are met;
- ensure that the Release Management process operates effectively and efficiently;
- ensure that Release Management staff are empowered in their jobs;

- maximize the fit between people, process, technology/tool and steering;
- establish the Release Manager and (Key-) Release Coordinators as the central and accepted point of contact for changes;
- ensure standardized methods and techniques are used for the preparation, building, testing and implementation to meet agreed service levels and prevent change-related incidents.

Activities
- coach (Key-)Process Coordinators in the correct use of the process;
- identify training requirements in the (virtual) team;
- identify improvement opportunities to ensure the process and tools are effective and efficient;
- function as a point of escalation for Release Coordinators;
- the Release Manager escalates to the Release Management Process Owner where the process is not fit-for-purpose. The Release Manager escalates to line management and the Release Management Process Owner in case of a conflict between process and line management. Escalation reports are sent to the Release Management Process Owner and line management;
- review whether and initiate appropriate action to ensure all parties involved are familiar with and follow the process, including external suppliers (contractors and vendors);
- promote and communicate the process to all parties involved;
- provide Release Management process staff with appropriate information to enable them to perform their function effectively;
- review and provide information for reports (produced by Release Manager Assistant/ Deputy);
- monitor and audit the process, using qualitative and quantitative Key Performance Indicators;
- schedule and attend meetings according to the process and governance structure.

Authorities
- report on all releases, specified per service, process, department, and any other Key Performance Indicator that will be established;
- escalate Service Level Agreement breaches to line management (where applicable directly to section managers) and process management;
- recommend service improvements.

Competencies and qualifications
The ideal Release Manager has the following competencies and qualifications:
- understanding of the services that IT delivers to the business and its users;
- both flexible and convincing, as they often do not have authority over staff working with the processes;
- ability to withstand pressure when needed;
- ITSM Foundation certificate and moving forward to achieve the relevant Practitioners Certificate;
- ability to coach and mentor process staff;
- general knowledge of IT;
- good knowledge of the organization;
- strong internal network;
- ability to act as a discussion partner for Director level and one level below.

Release Manager Assistant

Objective of the role
- assist the Release Manager in day-to-day operation of the process;
- sharing of workload of Release Manager;
- deputize for the Release Manager, when and if required, providing greater accessibility to the Release Management process.

Responsibilities
- assist with or carry out the activities delegated to him by the Release Manager, like producing fit-for-purpose and timely reports and reviews;
- understand the process, procedures, work instructions, policies, required documentation and tools.

Activities
- monitor, track, update and close the release records during appropriate points in the release life cycle (e.g. progress information);
- register, monitor and update the Forward Schedule of Releases (for planning purposes);
- review and report possible bottlenecks and issues regarding scheduled releases to the Release Manager;
- produce steering information in the shape of management reports based on the Key Performance Indicators (KPIs);
- report on releases to those involved according to Process governance structure on behalf of the Release Manager when required;
- assist with the audit of the Release Management process;
- provide and distribute reports regarding urgent (emergency) releases;
- provide and distribute escalation reports when required;
- provide information on and arrange training when required;
- assist with the promotion and communication of the process to all parties involved, through e.g. the maintenance of a web-page, info mails and bulletins where needed;
- liaise with the Release Coordinators and Workers when required;
- send invitations, prepare and attend meetings according to the Release Management process and governance structure when required;
- perform secretarial activities when required (e.g. minutes of meetings).

Authorities
- escalate and report to the Release Manager and when appropriate on behalf of the Release Manager to line management or process staff;
- recommend any improvements regarding processes, reporting, communication, training and tools.

Competencies and qualifications
The ideal Release Manager Assistant has the following competencies and qualifications:
- must be a good communicator;
- is a discussion partner for staff of all processes as well as Manager level and one level below;
- has good knowledge of Service Management and reporting tools;

- has a helicopter view on the activities required for Release Management process and the relationship with other processes;
- is flexible and convincing, as they often do not have authority over staff working with the process;
- knows the ICT organization well;
- must be both flexible and strong to withstand pressure when needed;
- knows how to 'get things done';
- possesses at least the ITSM Foundations certificate and is preferably moving forward to achieve the relevant Practitioners Certificate;
- has basic knowledge of the IT-infrastructure to determine the impact of releases and assesses where in the organizations the release will take place.

Release Management Process Coordinator

Objective of the role
- to establish a coordination function within the department or section in which they are working.
  NB: The Release Management Process Coordinator is not the same as the person who coordinates or implements the release itself. This is done by the Release Management Process Worker.

Responsibilities
- ensure that the Release Management process is applied correctly within the department/ section;
- seek communication with peer (Key-)Release Coordinators when required;
- be aware of the objectives and activities of all parties involved;
- coordinate release activities with other sections and/or departments;
- ensure the Release Management process, procedures, work instructions, and tools are optimal from a department/section point of view;
- ensure Release management Process Workers within the department or section are empowered to execute their tasks.

Activities
- propagate the (correct) use of the Release Management process within the department/ section;
- coordinate release activities with other Key Release Coordinators when needed;
- engage with other departments to keep an up-to-date view on their objectives and activities;
- coach the Release Management Process Workers in the correct use of process and tools;
- identify improvement opportunities within the department/section;
- assist the Release Manager to build the business case for an enhancement request and assist with the evaluation of releases (Post Implementation Reviews);
- identify specific training needs within the department, and signal these needs to section/ department manager and the Release Manager;
- communicate releases to the Release Management process within the department/section and promote the use of the changed process;
- identify possible bottlenecks and issues regarding scheduled changes within the department/ section and communicate them to the Release Manager (Assistant/Deputy);

- coordinating release activities during the various steps of release management, or taking care that the Release Worker coordinated all activities.

Depending on the size of the department and release itself, the Release Management Process Coordinator can also have an active role with the release itself.

Authorities
- escalate to the section line management in case of Service Level Agreement breaches;
- escalate to the Release Manager;
- monitor Implementation progress for all changes that were initiated within the department or that were dispatched by his department;
- the single point of contact within their department for escalations;
- initiate coordination meetings with other Release Coordinators when required.

Competencies and qualifications
The ideal Release Management Process Coordinator has the following competencies and qualifications:
- sufficient technical knowledge specific to his department to be able to understand the release and coordinate and control the release process;
- good communication skills;
- helicopter view on the activities of his own department;
- is a respected member of a department and is able to combine daily departmental activities with their coordination role;
- knows how to 'get things done';
- possesses an ITSM Foundation certificate;
- is delegated by his line manager to oversee process activities within the department.

General remarks on the Coordinator role
Not every department will need a Release Management Process Coordinator. The role does not have to be unique for one process; one Coordinator can have a role within multiple processes.

The position of the Release Management Process Coordinator is not a full-time position; however, a strong commitment during implementation of Release Management is required. Once the processes have been implemented, it is estimated that the role of Release Management Process Coordinator will require no more than 25 per cent of a 40-hour working week per process.

Release Management Process Workers
Objective of the role
The Release Management Process Worker role does not require the creation of specific objectives. Rather it is a role, adapted by any IT staff member, vendor or contractor whose (daily) activities involve the implementation of releases.

Responsibilities
- execute activities in adherence to the applicable procedures and instructions of the process.

Activities

Day-to-day activities of the Release Management Process Worker are very numerous. They depend very much on the type of release and the phase in which the implementation is in. With large release more than one release worker could be appointed, with one of them acting as a Project Manager. With small releases the release worker could actually perform the activities himself.

A few examples of Release Management Process Worker tasks are given below:
- designing, building and configuring the release or taking care that this is done;
- testing the release or taking care that this has been done;
- producing an exact, detailed timetable of events, as well as who will do what (i.e. a resource plan) or taking care that this is done;
- communicate, train (if applicable) staff and/or end-users involved or taking care that this is done;
- distributing and installing the implementation or taking care that this is done.

General activities regarding the Release Management process include:
- identify opportunities for improvement;
- obtain the technical and organizational knowledge required to perform the activities;
- monitor and provide progress information on the scheduled releases they are working on when required;
- identify possible bottlenecks and issues regarding scheduled releases and communicate them to the Release Coordinator;
- escalate to the Release Coordinator if required;
- create management reports.

Authorities
- signal and escalate (horizontally or vertically) Service Level Agreement breaches for releases;
- deny any pressure to by-pass the Release Management process;
- escalate and/or indicate a need for more training and/or technical and organizational information.

Competencies and qualifications
- specific competencies or qualifications can be not given for Release Management Process Workers. This totally depends on the type and size of the release in question;
- good understanding of the Release Management process;
- general understanding of operational ITSM processes and their relationships.

Definitive Software Librarian
Objective of the role
The objective of this role is to:
- establish an administrative function for the day-to-day management of the Definitive Software Library.

Responsibilities
The responsibilities of this role are to:
• maintain libraries or other storage areas to hold software;
• maintain software according to the set procedures;
• report to the Release Manager about issues regarding the DSL.

Activities
The activities associated with this role are to:
• supervise and control receipt, identification, storage and withdrawal of all original software in DSL.
• lend working copies out according to set procedures;
• maintain and provide information on the status of the software (versions);
• assist in conducting audits.

Competencies and qualifications
• must be a good communicator;
• has good knowledge of the Release Management process and its relationship with the DSL.
• must be both flexible and strong to withstand pressure when needed.
• possesses an ITSM Foundation certificate;
• has basic knowledge of the IT-infrastructure to understand the software maintained in the DSL and understand the reason for some questions about them.

6.6.2 Release procedures
What activities need to be executed and by whom when a release is being implemented?
Release Management consists of the following process steps:
• prepare and plan release;
• designing, building and/or configuring;
• testing;
• roll-out planning;
• communication, preparation and/or training;
• distribution and installation.

Each of the process steps is described in: objectives, input, procedure and output.

Process step 1: Prepare and plan release
Objectives
Prepare and plan all activities during the other phases of the release process.

Input
Release planning input includes:
• authorized RFC;
• CAB output (additional remarks from CAB from discussing RFC in meeting);
• release Policy;
• qualified staff: technical skills on topic of release, but also understanding of business to understand impact on service.

Procedure

Activities	Involved process role
Coordinate appointment release worker	Release Manager, Release Assistant, Release Process Coordinator, Department or Section Director, Team leader
Verify and update RFC information	Release Worker
Technical & Functional acceptance criteria present? This is needed for step 2 and 3.	Release Worker
No, Contact requestor	Release Worker
Make release planning	Release Worker
Plan resources for release	Release Worker, Department Managers/ Section Directors/ Team leaders
Purchase required?	Release Worker
Yes, start and manage purchase process	Release Worker, Requestor of RFC, Budget Holder
Make a test plan (including resourcing) Prepare step 3.	Release Worker, Department Managers/ Section Directors/ Team leaders
Discuss release with Configuration Management If, how, when and who will change CIs in CMDB?	Release Worker
Plan communication and training	Release Worker
Update call, release document and inform Release Coordinator	Release Worker

Table 6.5   Release Planning Procedure

Output
Release planning outputs include:
- the release planning, test plans;
- acceptance criteria for the release;
- purchased software and/or hardware or delivery date for these.

Process step 2: Designing, building and/or configuring
Objectives
Know exactly which steps need to be taken to implement release into the live environment.

Input
- RFC;
- technical en functional specification;
- planning;
- software and/or hardware;
- release document.

Procedure

Description	Involved process role
Training required?	Release Worker & RFC Requestor
Yes, Organize training	Release Worker
Put (original) software in DSL	Release Worker
Design, build, configure	Release Worker
Automated script required for implementation?	Release Worker
Yes, create script for automated roll-out?	Release Worker
Write instructions All steps taken to design, build or configure the release, need to be documented. They will be needed for testing, implementation in live environment, solve incidents, problems or as a basis for future updates.	Release Worker
Create roll-back plan	Release Worker
Re-assess impact analyses of change process	Release Worker
Update call, release document and inform Release Coordinator	Release Worker

Table 6.6   Implementation Procedure

Output
- detailed instructions on how to design, build or configure the release;
- roll-back plan.

Process step 3: Testing

Objectives

The objective is to prevent releases from adversely impacting on service levels or service quality. Testing can also save time and money, because (in practice) it often turns out that the effort and costs for rectifying an implemented release are greater than the effort and costs involved in testing a release.

Although recommended, it is not always possible or justifiable to fully test all releases in advance. For urgent changes, for instance, there is often not enough time for testing before implementation. It may be possible to (also) use modeling techniques to assess the likely impact (e.g. expected network traffic and affect on capacity and performance). When a release is not or not completely tested this should be specifically mentioned in all communication.

Input
- rest plan;
- independent tester; for ensuring objective testing, it is recommended that the Tester is not the same person as the Builder;
- policy;
- test environment identical to live environment;
- change testing policy document.

Procedure

Description	Involved process role
Perform technical test	Release Worker
Technical test OK?	Release Worker
No, return to step 2	Release Worker
Yes, perform functional test	Release Worker
Functional test OK?	Release Worker
No, return to step 2	Release Worker
Yes, test roll-back plan	Release Worker
Test roll-back OK?	Release Worker
No, return to step 2	Release Worker
Register all test results	Release Worker
Update call, release document and inform Release Coordinator	Release Worker

Table 6.7   Testing procedure

Output
• Documented results of functional, technical and roll-back tests.

NB: A Final Acceptance test is done after step 6.

Step 4: Roll-out planning
Objectives
Roll-out planning extends the overall release plan from step 1, to add details of the exact installation process developed and the agreed implementation plan.

Input
• high level release planning (from step 1);
• details from RFC;
• additional information obtained during release process;
• release document.

Procedure

Description	Involved process role
Make list of CI to change Important during roll-out, but also useful for informing the Configuration Management process.	Release Worker
Hardware replaced?	Release Worker
Yes, make plan to dispose redundant hardware? This will become part of the roll-out plan.	Release Worker
Downtime needed?	Release Worker
Request downtime Follow procedure for requesting downtime.	Release Worker
Roll-out to multiple locations?	Release Worker

Description	Involved process role
Yes, choose roll-out method Phased roll-out or big bang approach.	Release Worker
No, produce release notes and communications	Release Worker
Make detailed roll-out plan	Release Worker
Update call & release document and inform Release Coordinator	Release Worker

Table 6.8   Roll-out planning procedure

Output
- exact, detailed timetable of events;
- who is doing what?
- list of CIs;
- permission for downtime;
- release notes (if applicable).

Step 5: Communication, preparation and/or training
Objectives
Inform all people that will or could be affected by the implementation of the release.

Input
- release notes;
- communication details;
- known-errors.

Procedure

Description	Involved process role
Communication required?	Release Worker
Yes, send out communication	Release Worker
Training required?	Release Worker
Yes, organize training	Release Worker
Inform known errors to Problem Management	Release Worker
Update call & release document and inform Release Coordinator	Release Worker

Table 6.9   Communication & training procedure

Output
- informed relevant users/IT staff;
- trained IT staff;
- known errors to Problem Management.

Step 6: Distribution and installation
Objectives
Implement the release into the live environment with least possible interruption of the service levels.

Input
- detailed roll-out plan;
- tested installation procedures;

- tested release components;
- rested roll-back plan.

Procedure

Description	Involved process role
Release Install, distribute and/or configure new release in the live environment according to roll-out plan	Release Worker
Data migration required?	Release Worker
Yes, data migration	Release Worker
No, roll-back required?	Release Worker
Yes, roll-back	Release Worker
Final Acceptance Test if applicable	Release Worker
CMDB change Or give input to Configuration Management on	Release Worker
Return working copy to DSL	Release Worker, DSL Librarian
Update call & release document and inform Release Coordinator	Release Worker

Table 6.10   Distribution and installation procedure

Output
- An updated IT service, with updated User and support documentation;
- Updated CMDB records to reflect new live components;
- Decommissioned CIs (such as redundant software and hardware).

6.6.3 DSL Design
Management of the Definitive Software Library (DSL) is one of the repetitive tasks of Release Management. This paragraph describes the design of the DSL. It will describe how it is set up, how and how long the software will be stored and how other people can access it.

Purpose of the DSL
The purpose of the DSL is to maintain a secure and suitable place to store and control the master copies of all controlled software. The DSL should include definitive copies of purchased software (along with license documents or information), as well as software developed on site.
Due to the size and spread of the system, the need might arise for another DSL. The need and approval for this will have to be judged by the Release Manager. It is advisable to limit the number of DSL as much as possible. The procedures, work instructions and policies described in this document should be used for all software libraries.

Scope of the DSL
The following software will be stored in the DSL when it adheres to the policies mentioned in chapter 2:
- master copies of licensed software that have been purchased from vendors;
- master copies of Alpha version of in-house developed software that have been implemented;
- license documents of purchased software packages.

Not part of the DSL will be:

- manuals related to the software: these can be handed over to the electronic library department;
- any software that was not released in the live environment (for example: Beta version of in-house developed software). See also the following paragraph.

Starting-up phase and development of the DSL in the future

At the set up of a DSL, a lot of software is, of course, already in the live environment. This means that new software will not only enter the DSL via the Release Management process (when it has been officially approved by the CAB).

Software will also be handed over to the DSL directly by IT staff, who had the software in their 'own' libary. This is very typical for the setup phase of the DSL.

Having no CMDB available at the setup phase, the DSL Librarian will have to store this information temporarily on an Excel spreadsheet. A template for this is available at the end of this section.

Relationships with other IT Processes

Change Management

New software is implemented under the authority of the Change Management process. This will mean that before software is stored in the DSL, it will already be authorized by the CAB.

Configuration Management

Software can only be entered in the DSL when it is registered as Configuration Item in the CMDB. The CMDB will also supply the numbering of the software.

When the status of the software is changed in the DSL due to entry of a newer version or due to the policies on retention, this information will be passed on to the Configuration Manager.

Standardization of software versions

Having only one version of a software package in the live environment is a goal that should be pursued by the entire IT department. It will, in general, improve stability and make implementing changes a lot easier.

Having one DSL with policies on lending out software can assist the IT department in this goal. In the start-up phase of the DSL this goal should not be pursued too vigorously. It will stop IT staff from handing over their software to the DSL.

Standardization of software is not the sole responsibility of DSL or Release Management!

Making software online available

Part of the purpose of the DSL is to make the software available to IT staff who need it. This can be done in two ways:
- **physically** - by borrowing a copy of the original software;
- **digitally** - by giving access to the installation files on a DSL file server.

Policies and requirements for the DSL

Policy for storing software in DSL

Retention policy: One old version of all DSL software will be stored with the original DSL item. Older versions will be thrown away.

There is no limit to the time that a user can borrow software from the DSL. The term will be registered and a mechanism is place to note late return.

Software with an 'archived' status, is only lent out under the specific agreement of a manager. It will not be put in the all-users folder on the file server.

Requirements to the physical DSL
- fire proof vault;
- access only by DSL Librarian or after his approval.

Naming and numbering convention for software
- CD stored in the DSL will be numbered and labeled <DSLXXXX>;
- XXXX is a consecutive number.; the next available number can be derived from the overview sheet;
- if one jewel box contains more than one CD, each CD will get one number;
- working copies should be numbered and labeled <DSLXXXXW> (where XXXX is, of course, the same as the original);
- the CDs will also be stored in this order so that it will be easy to find them;
- A number is never to be re-used again.

Authorization
The form to borrow software from the DSL needs to be signed by two people:
- the Manager of the person who wants to borrow the software;
- the Release Manager. If they are not present the Release Owner or the Release Assistant are authorized to sign it.

Procedures and work instructions

Receiving and storing
- register on Excel spreadsheet;
- label received software according to naming convention;
- put software in vault;
- send email as receipt of software;
- make work copy if necessary for short term.

Lending out
- check request for completeness and authorization;
- make working copy of original CD and number it according to naming convention;
- send working copy to requestor;
- register lending out in excel overview.

Return after lending out
Working copy:
1. take in working copy;
2. change registration;
3. store working copy with original.

Removal of software from DSL
1. check if removal is in accordance with policy and obtain approval from release manager;
2. remove software from vault;
3. remove software from server, including user group and directory;
4. change registration.

Detection and retrieval of not-returned software
1. verify every week on the overview sheet software that has not been returned;
2. send an email to user;
3. if user does not react send an email to their manager;
4. if manager does not react after one week, escalate this issue to the Release Manager Assistant.

Reporting
Send a monthly report to the Release Manager and his assistant with the following information:
1. list of software that was put in;
2. list of software that was archived;
3. list of software that was disposed of;
4. issues and queries.

Template: Form for lending out software

Date:

COMPUTER DEPARTMENT   **DEFINITIVE SOFTWARE LIBRARY**

Details of CDs to be Borrowed:

CD number(s)	
CD Description	

Borrowers Details:

Name:	Depart./sectn.
ID. No. /Phone #:	

Department	Fin □ IT □ Admin □	Othrs: specify

Dept. Head:	Phone #:

Department Head Signature: (if the borrower is not from MAS staff)	Approved □ Disapproved □

Approval by Release Management	Name:	Signature:

Borrowed on: Borrower's sign Signature of the Librarian   Signature of the Librarian

			Estimated return date:	
			Returned on:	

REMARKS:

Template: Overview sheet

Number	Name+Version	Supplier	Status	Resposible Department/Section	Contact	Date entered/ status change	User group	Lend out to	Lend out untill

6.6.4   Release Management Operational Level Agreement

Replace all red lettering with the appropriate content and change the font color to 'automatic' to customize the agreement for your situation.

Release Management **Operational Level Agreement**
This agreement is made between the Release Manager, *<insert the name of the Release Manager>* and *<insert the title and name of the IT manager or representative>*.
This agreement covers the *<insert the IT group name>*'s participation in and support of the IT Release Management process.
In order to ensure consistent delivery of Release Management services, the following objectives are guaranteed for release related services performed by *<insert the name of the IT group or team>*. (*The following are some examples*) All release management activity will be performed according to the Release Policy. A Release Coordinator will be designated for the team. Release Management Process Worker will be assigned to releases within 24 hours of the request. All release activity will be recorded and tracked in the enterprise release tool. At least one team representative will attend the weekly release meeting, *held <insert time/date/location of meetings>*, either in person or via telephone conference. *<Insert any other applicable objectives.>*
This agreement remains valid until replaced by a revised agreement mutually endorsed by the agreeing parties indicated below.
This agreement will be reviewed every six months, but can be changed at any time as agreed by the parties indicated below.
Name: Position: Date:
Name: Release Manager: Date:

6.6.5 Communication Plan Template

Stakeholders	Message	What's in it for them? (WIIFM)	Who should deliver the message?	Media/Format	Timing	Reinforcement /Reminder

Considerations for completing the Communication Plan Template:
- **Stakeholders:**
  - Consider all stakeholders for the project or process.
  - Typical stakeholders include IT executives, customers, managers, IT staff, users.
  - Consider if the stakeholders can be grouped for one message or if they require different messages/formats and thus require a unique approach (i.e. Service Desk IT staff may get one message while the 2nd/3rd level support team may need a different view).
- **Message:**
  - Define the goal of the message (i.e. solicit participation in the pilot program).
  - Different messages will be needed throughout the initiative, list each communication required.
  - Consider what action you want to result from the communication or what you want the receivers to think and/or feel as a result of the communication.
- **WIIFM:**
  - Consider what this communication means to the receivers and why would they be interested or how they will be affected.
- **Who should deliver the message?:**
  - Consider who should deliver/send the message for the most significant impact.
- **Media/Format:**
  - Identify the most effective format for delivering this message to this stakeholder group.
  - Consider existing formats such as regular team meetings, newsletters, regular executive meetings, etc.
  - Also consider if the message needs to be distinguished from other communications with some unique format such as a hard-copy mailing, flyer, etc.
- **Timing:**
  - Consider the appropriate timing of the message.
  - Plan for dependencies (i.e. the management team may need to be aware of a message prior to the staff, etc)
- **Reinforcement/reminder:**
  - Consider if a follow-up communication will be required or if there be some sort of take-away from a meeting to remind the receiver of the message.

6.6.6 Training Plan Template

Purpose

The purpose of the *<insert process name>* Training Plan is to ensure preparedness for: *<insert the description of the release>*

Target Audience

The target audiences are:

Role	Quantity to be trained
End users	*<insert number of people to be trained here>*
Technical support staff	
Service Desk staff	
<insert other roles>	

Training Modules

The following table describes the specific training to support the implementation of *<insert the release name>* into the environment. *<enter the descriptions of the training to address the training needs of all the target audiences identified in the section above>*

Module Name	Objectives	Delivery Method	Length	Pre-reqs	Target Audience
Insert training module name	Outline training objectives here	Identify format of training (lecture, hands-on, on-line, one-on-one, etc	Enter the length of training	Identify any pre-requisite activities to be completed here	List the target audience members from the chart above

Training Schedule

In order to meet the needs of the project plan, the following training schedule applies:

Module	# of Sessions	Dates	Notes
Insert module name from list above	Insert the # of sessions to be offered if applicable	Dates training is to be offered	Include size limits, enrollment instructions, etc

6.7   Knowledge test questions

Question 1
Which of the following items will not be found in the DSL?
A. Functional Design of a business application
B. Spare parts
C. A baseline laptop image
D. Program Source Code

Question 2
What is the role of the Definitive Software Library (DSL) in the Release Management process?
A. (Physical) Storage of the original versions of all software used
B. Reference work containing all software documentation manuals, etc.
C. Registration tool for all software items
D. Sort of Configuration Management Database (CMDB) for software

Question 3
Which activity is part of the Release Management process?
A. Approving a change in Application X from version 1 to version 1.1
B. Put together the release containing the new version 1.1 of Application X
C. To record which computers the new version 1.1 of Application X is installed on

Question 1
At which moment does Release Management start building, testing and implementing a change?
A. As soon as the members of the Change Advisory Board (CAB) have discussed the impact analysis
B. As soon as the Request for Change (RFC) has been formally authorized and the planning has been set
C. As soon as the Service Quality Plan has been updated to warrant the quality after the execution of the change
D. As soon as Problem Management files the RFC

6.8   Practical assignments

Description
Improvement plan for the Release Management process. A documented Release Management process is available.

Goals
1. Describe the present Release Management process.
2. Define KPIs.
3. Compile first concept for KPI reporting.
4. Compile customer reports.

Implementation

The implementation consists of the following stages:

1. Description of present working methods (2 hours).
2. Define KPIs (2 hours).

7 Change Management

7.1 Introduction

To ensure the smooth supply of IT services – in line with the business processes of the customer, it is essential that changes are implemented without introducing faults and that the changes are made for the right reasons. The risks associated with all changes also have to be minimized.

Most Requests For Change (RFC) that result in improvements or corrections to the infrastructure may not only originate from Problem Management; IT service customers may also make changes – via RFCs or by unauthorized approaches. Such changes often lead to new disruptive incidents and further challenges. Change Management's job is to break this cycle by enforcing conscious decision taking and controlling all changes whilst minimizing risk.

7.1.1 Rationale of Change Management

Each change to the existing delivery infrastructure represents a potential threat to the stability of the IT services currently being delivered.

All changes must be controlled. This can be done by introducing and using standardized methods and procedures. By doing so, the risk of the IT service provision being interrupted by a change to a CI is minimized.

It is very important to keep a balance between stability and flexibility when it comes to considering changes. A strict change procedure helps to maintain the stability of the system whilst allowing the flexibility needed for implementing 'an urgent RFC'.

The change process must be 'fit for purpose'. The checks and balances required must reflect the risk, cost, and scope of the changes that are being managed. Change Management must be viewed as 'the best way' and 'the only way' to introduce new components into the production environment.

7.1.2 Definition of a 'Change'

A change is defined as the addition, modification or removal of approved, supported or baselined hardware, network, software, application, environment, system, personnel or documentation.

Not every change to the infrastructure will be formally regarded as a change; a defined and agreed scoping document showing what is and what is not covered by Change Management will be one of the initial deliverables to be created during the implementation planning process.

Changes that entail a modification in the status of one or more CIs, must always be made via Change Management. The concept of a change and how the change is to be managed must be clearly defined and consistently followed. Optimizing the change process requires that all CIs that are subject to change are recorded in the CMDB. Each change which leads to a new status for one or more CIs is regarded as a change to the IT infrastructure. This must include the introduction of any new item.

7.1.3 Roles and Responsibilities of Change Management

The following roles may be considered. A detailed description of these roles can be found in the sample 'Change Management Roles' at the end of this chapter.

- **Change Requestor** - A requestor is responsible for the initiation of a change and the registration and submittance of an RFC.

- **Change Coordinator** - The Change Coordinator has 'end-to-end' responsibility for a change.
- **Change Project Leader** - One or more project leaders can be assigned for managing specific activities or phases of a change which are handled as projects, e.g. a build phase, a test phase, an implementation phase. A Change Project Leader will report to the Change Coordinator.
- **Change Handler** - The Change Handler is responsible for the realization of specific activities in a change (e.g. plan, build, test, implement) and will report to the Project Leader or the Change Coordinator.
- **Change Reviewer** - The role of Change Reviewer is to ensure that the change, as defined in the RFC database, is reviewed properly after successful implementation and sign-off by the Change Handler/Project Leader.
- **Change Advisory Board (CAB)** - This board is responsible for the assessment of all changes with the exception of standard changes, and advises the Change Manager on the handling of changes.
- **Change Manager** - The Change Manager is the person accountable for all activities and results of the Change Management process.

7.2   Topics & theory 'Manage'

7.2.1   Change Advisory Board

The Change Advisory Board (CAB) is a body that helps Change Management in the assessing, prioritizing and approving of changes. The CAB members should be key stakeholders in the change; they will have the capability and competence to ensure that all changes that impact their domain are adequately assessed from business, technical and support viewpoints.

Under normal conditions, CAB membership would be made up of:
- change Manager
- customer representatives
- user management
- user group representative team leads
- application developers/maintainers
- experts/technical consultants
- office services staff
- vendors (if involved - for instance in outsourcing situations).

Membership in CAB may vary from meeting to meeting, depending on the changes that require approval. CAB membership will generally have a core of regular attendees, but will need to co-opt other staff when specific skills and opinions are required.

In general, CAB attendees:
- will be selected according to the changes being considered;
- may vary considerably in skills and opinions even during a single CAB meeting;
- should involve suppliers (internal or external);
- should reflect supplier, user, customer and business views; and
- will generally will include the Problem Manager, Service Level Manager and Customer Relations staff.

When major incidents arise, and a change is required to solve the incident, there may not be time to convene the full CAB; in this case a smaller organization known as the CAB Emergency Comittee (CAB/EC) has the authority to make quick and considered decisions on what must be done to recover from the major incident. Other urgent changes will be subject to such a CAB/EC as well. Change procedures should specify the composition of the CAB and CAB/EC; the composition will be based on the criteria listed above and other criteria appropriate to the business. The CAB/EC must have the expertise to ensure that critical changes are assessed, built, tested and implemented with the minimum delay.

7.3   Topics & theory 'Organize'

7.3.1   Change Procedure
Change Management procedures will help coordinate the various people and organizations who work together to implement a change. The procedure for a change varies from organization to organization, but on the whole, certain phases are common and can be defined.
- **RFC acceptance** - Issued RFC's are received by Change Management and checked for completeness, formulation, scope, financing, etcetera. Change Management helps with obtaining completeness and clearness of all issued RFC. An RFC must contain sufficient information to understand the exact nature of the change. This phase is concluded with a decision to go ahead with the change (formal acceptance).
- **Assessment and Planning** - The implications of an RFC are assessed, the build, test and implementation of the change are planned. This phase is concluded with a decision to authorize the requested change.
- **Building** - After a positive decision, the item can be built. The build phase could also involve the acquisition of equipment and software.
- **Testing** - Once the item has been built, it is tested. If there are any problems at this stage, the item goes back to the building phase. Ideally there should be 'zero defects'; however when tests show that any faults are 'within tolerance' then the CIs can be implemented. Ideally Service Desk staff should contribute to the test phase. This phase is concluded with a decision to implement the item in the live environment.
- **Implementation** - The accepted item is implemented, according to the approved implementation plan. At this stage, other parties, such as the Service Desk and, if necessary, users, must be informed. Should the implementation not be successful, the system should revert back to its previous version. The RFC is reassessed and new plans made.
- **Review** - After the changed CIs have been in use for an agreed period, they must be reviewed. The review may lead to further requests to repair new faults that have emerged or to improve the level of service.
- **Closure** - The changes are only regarded as completed when evaluation shows that the intended results have been achieved and that the implementation was carried out successfully. If the change was made to correct a known error, this recorded error can also be regarded as repaired. Closure of the change should also involve a check with Configuration Management to ensure that all changes are registered correctly.

7.3.2 Activities

As well as managing the change processes and procedures, Change Management is responsible for managing the interfaces between itself and the other business and IT functions.

The main activities of Change Management include:
- Plan the implementation of operational procedures
- Log and filter changes
- Allocate change priorities
- Categorize changes
- Manage CAB meetings
- Assess impact and resource
- Approve changes
- Schedule changes
- Build, test and implement changes
- Review changes
- Provide management reports and other change related information.

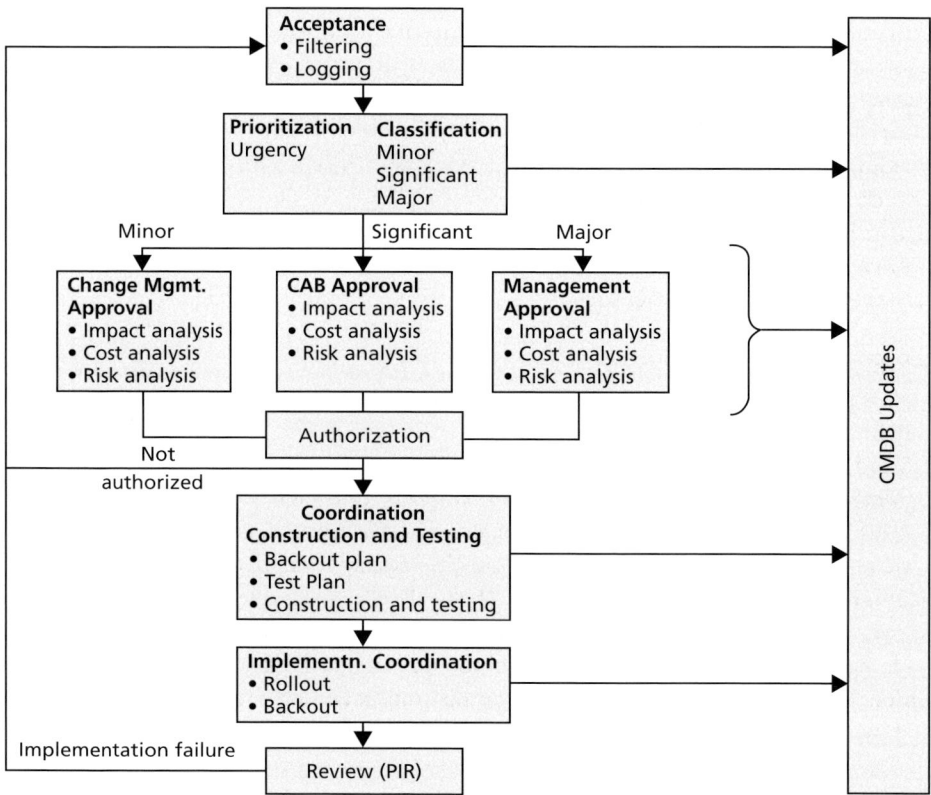

Figure 7.1   Change procedure

7.3.3   Plan the implementation of operational procedures

Change Management should plan the implementation of operational procedures for the activities described in this section, or amend any existing procedures to help ensure that they conform to these guidelines.

7.3.4   Log and filter changes

All RFCs received should be logged and allocated an identification number (in chronological sequence). Where change requests are submitted as a resolution to a problem record (PR), than the original PR number must be retained so that the link between the problem and its resolution is recognized and understood.

Ideally, the logging of RFCs is made via an integrated Service Management tool. This should be capable of storing both the data on all CIs and also, importantly, the relationships between them. This will help to assess the likely impact of a change to one component of the system on all other components. All actions should be recorded, as they are carried out, within the Change Management log. If this is not possible at the time, then they should be manually recorded for inclusion at the earliest opportunity.

Procedures shall specify who has access to the logging system and what the levels of access will be. Normally, access to the system is open to authorized personnel, typical 'authorized personnel' are restricted to those who need to create, or add reports of progress to an RFC. Note that the support tool should also keep Change Management aware of such actions. Only Change Management staff (or Configuration Management support staff if Change Management is an integral part of a Configuration Management system) should be allowed to close an RFC.

The procedures should stipulate that, as changes are logged, Change Management should briefly consider each request and filter out any that are totally impractical. The RFC should be returned to the initiator, together with brief details of the reason for the rejection, and the log should record what actions were taken and why. A right of appeal against rejection should exist; how to appeal is described within the procedures.

7.3.5   Allocate change priorities

Every RFC should be allocated a *priority*. The priority is based on the impact of the problem and the urgency for the remedy. The priority rating is used to decide which changes should be discussed and assessed first, either by Change Management or with the assistance of the CAB. Change Management should be responsible for assigning the priority. The priority of RFCs should be decided in collaboration with the initiator and, if necessary, with the CAB. It should not be left to the initiator alone, as a higher priority than is really justified may result. Risk assessment is of crucial importance at this stage. The CAB will need information on the potential business consequences in order to assess the risk of implementing or denying the change.

RFCs will have already been annotated with the priority defined and agreed within the organization. The priority will depend mainly on the impact and urgency of the problem. The priority shows the order in which they should be 'fixed'. This code should be reviewed and (unless there is a good reason not to) should be used as a basis for the change priority. Timeframes for each priority level should be predetermined and escalation processes defined.

7.3.6   Categorize changes

The issue of risk to the business of any change should also be considered before the *approval* of any change. Change Management should examine each RFC and decide how to proceed, based on the (predefined) *category* into which the RFC falls. The categorization process examines the impact of the approved change on the organization in terms of the resources needed to make the change. Note that the structure and complexity of these categories will usually depend on the needs of the business, including the range of priority ratings identified.

Example categories are set out below. It is expected that the majority of RFCs will fall into the example categories 'minor' and 'significant'.

Each of these categories could be given a number. Numbering systems vary between service support tools and are subject to local considerations. Two examples are given below:

0- standard change
1- minor impact
2- significant impact
3- major impact

or

1- major impact
2- significant impact
3- minor impact
4- standard change

Minor impact only, and few additional resources required

Change Management should have delegated authority to authorize and schedule such changes, but these should be logged so that:

• records and work patterns can be identified – and ideally work packages allocated;
• accurate and complete costs for each service, customer area, etc. impacted, can be determined;
• repetitive changes, follow-on changes, and associated problem/incident areas can be identified.

In summary, recording every change helps to deliver an effective and efficient service to the customer by allowing wastefully repetitive tasks to be spotted and eliminated. If Change Management has any doubts about authorizing any such change, the change can be referred informally to members of the CAB for a broader assessment.

Significant impact and/or significant resources required

Depending on the urgency of the change to be made, Change Management should decide whether to review these with the CAB or to convene a CAB/EC. Prior to any meeting, all documentation should be circulated for impact and resource assessment.

Major impact and/or very large amount of resources required, or impact likely upon other parts of the organization

Where a major change pertains directly to IT, the RFC should be referred to the organization's top Management Board or other appropriate body for discussion and a policy decision. Such changes, once approved should be passed back, perhaps via the CAB, for scheduling and implementation.

Standard change

Some modifications to the IT services (or infrastructure) may be completely standardized, cause low-risk, but are requested at a frequent base. This type of change could be categorized as a "standard change", to be handled in a predefined way (see paragraph 7.4 Optimize). If possible, these standard changes are handled by appropriate functions in the IT organization (Service Desk, Operations team). A simple registration may be required to support the change process and to inform the CAB.

7.3.7 Manage CAB meetings

CAB meetings should be prepared, and involved staff should be invited. An agenda should be sent out in time, so participants can prepare themselves for the changes to be discussed. Default representatives should consider bringing along experts to discuss changes that require extra expertise. A CAB agenda can contain several sections, e.g. Changes Implemented since last CAB, Standard Changes scheduled for implementation, New Changes to be discussed, Changes in progress.
A Forward Schedule of Changes should be made available to the CAB.
A CAB is normally chaired by the Change Manager.

7.3.8 Assess impact and resource

Each change is assessed for its impact and resource consumption:
- the impact that the change will make upon the customer's business operation;
- the effect upon the infrastructure and customer service, as defined in the SLA, and upon the capacity and performance, reliability and resilience, contingency plans, and security;
- the impact on other services that run on the same infrastructure (or on software development projects);
- the effect of not implementing the change;
- the IT, business and other resources required to implement the change, covering the likely costs, the number and availability of people required, the elapsed time, and any new infrastructure elements required;
- the current FSCs and PSAs; and any
- additional ongoing resources required if the change is implemented.

CAB recommendations

CAB members should come to meetings prepared to make decisions regarding which changes should go ahead, based on the priority assessment of the changes. The CAB should be informed of any changes that have been implemented as a workaround to incidents and should be given the opportunity to recommend follow-up action to these.
Note that the CAB is an advisory body only. If the CAB cannot agree to a recommendation, the final decision on whether to authorize changes, and commit to the expense involved, is the responsibility of management (normally the Director of IT or the Service Manager, or the Change Manager as their delegated representative). The Change Management procedures should specifically name the appointed person(s) authorized to sign off RFCs. Note that names are liable to change frequently. Depending on the nature of the change, references to Service Level Agreements may be required. In any event, customer sign-off will be required at some point.

7.3.9   Approve changes

Formal approval should be obtained for each change from the change authority. The change authority may be Change Management, the Service Manager, or some other appointed person or group. For low risk changes, the change authority may choose to be informed of changes authorized rather than be involved in authorizing each change individually. The levels of approval for a change should be judged by the size or risk of the change. For example, changes in a large enterprise that affect several distributed groups may need to be approved by a higher-level change authority.

There are three principal approval processes that should be in place in the Change Management process: financial approval, technical approval and business approval. Financial approval indicates that the cost of a change has been assessed and that it is either within approved budgetary limits or meets cost-benefit criteria that may have been set for change approval. The technical approval stage is an assurance that the change is feasible, sensible and can be performed without inappropriate detriment to the services provided to the business. If the technical experts are required to provide cost estimates (as is the case in many organizations), then this phase needs to precede financial approval. Customer approval is necessary to ensure that the business managers are content with the change proposals and the impact on their business requirements.

7.3.10 Schedule changes

Although it may be better (or advisable) to implement one change at a time—for example, in order to simplify diagnosis should an error occur—this is not usually practical. For instance, a hardware change may require an operating system change to support it; applications software may need to be changed so rapidly that a policy of "one change at a time" is impracticably slow; or a simple software change may require simultaneous introduction of new documentation, procedures *and* training.

Wherever possible, Change Management should schedule approved changes into target releases and recommend the allocation of resources accordingly. There is clear continuity between the Change Management and Release Management processes. Release Management processes impact upon the Change Management process and, in particular, have a role in developing and maintaining standard changes that introduce new or revised software and hardware into the infrastructure. As releases are the deliverables from changes, the change process initiates the releases under the agreed, documented and maintained release process.

It is recommended that Change Management issue the Forward Schedule of Changes (FSCs). FSCs should include details of all changes that have been authorized for implementation over a previously agreed (with the business) period, and the release(s) that they have been allocated to. Note that some organizations will have clear plans for the short term and less detailed plans in the longer term, however all plans must be included in the FSC. Brief details of (probably major) changes planned for the next two years should also be included. The FSC should be distributed to all customers and users or their representatives, application developers, service staff including the Service Desk, and any other interested parties. Distribution of FSCs outside Service Management should be done via the Service Desk or customer liaison process.

7.3.11 Build, test and implement changes

Authorized RFCs should be passed to the relevant technical groups involved in building the changes. This might involve:
• building a new production module;

- creating a new version of one or more software modules;
- purchasing equipment or services externally;
- preparing a hardware modification;
- producing new or amended documentation;
- preparing amendments to user training.

Change Management has a coordination role (supported by Release Management and normal line management controls) to ensure that these activities are both resourced and also completed to schedule. Release Management has a more important role in implementing smaller changes, such as when application software development teams provide Configuration Management installation and back-out instructions/files.

It is important to ensure that the same standards and methods that were used for building an original component are again used for the change. Back-out procedures should be prepared and documented in advance, before implementing the authorized change, so that if errors occur after implementation, the back-out procedures can be quickly activated with minimum impact on service quality.

To prevent changes from adversely impacting on service quality, all changes should be thoroughly tested in advance (including back-out procedures where possible). Testing should include aspects of the change such as:

- performance;
- security;
- internal and external maintainability;
- reliability/availability;
- functionality.

This advice is particularly relevant to the desktop environment, where constant technology updates take place. In many cases, this will require a separate "test environment". It may not always be possible or justifiable to fully test all changes in advance, however by using modeling techniques the decision on what, whether and how to test is made much simpler.

7.3.12 Review changes (Post-implementation review - PIR)

Change Management must review all implemented changes after a predefined period has elapsed. This process may still involve CAB members; Change Management may look to them for assistance in the review process. Change Management must review all implemented changes after a predefined period has elapsed. This process may still involve CAB members; Change Management may require their assistance in the review process.

Change reviews may be discussed at CAB meetings with agreement on any follow-up actions needed.

7.3.13 Provide management reports and other change related information

Potential metrics that relate to the success of the Change Management process are:

- Percentage of failed changes
- Percentage of rejected RFCs
- Number of unauthorized changes
- Change backlog
- Outages during changes

• Number of failed changes with no back-out plan
• Percentage of changes on time
• Percentage of changes causing incidents
• Number of CAB items not actioned on time
• Customer Satisfaction
• Number of emergency changes

Statistics that could be collected for management information are:
• Implemented changes by category
• Implemented changes by customer
• Implemented changes by system
• Number of known errors repaired
• Number of incidents repaired with a change
• Input from staff and resources
• Costs related to changes.

7.3.14 Forward Schedule of Change - FSC

The FSC is a schedule that contains details of all the changes approved for implementation and their proposed implementation dates. The FSC should be agreed with the customers and the business, Service Level Management, the Service Desk and Availability Management. Once agreed, the Service Desk should follow the defined communications strategy to ensure the user community is aware of any planned additional downtime and associated user implications arising from implementing the changes.

7.3.15 Change Calendar

A Change Calendar has been recognized in practice as a valuable instrument to support te planning of RFCs into an FSC. It differs from an FSC in that it describes the windows available for changes, and the types of changes that can be implemented in each window. The calendar is designed to assist both Change Requestors and CAB to perform initial change scheduling by making all parties aware of approved dates for change implementation.

7.3.16 Urgent changes

The number of urgent proposed changes should be kept to an absolute minimum, because they are generally more disruptive and prone to failure. All changes likely to be required should, in general, be foreseen and planned, bearing in mind the availability of resources to build and test the changes.
Nevertheless, occasions will occur when urgent changes are essential, so procedures should be devised to deal with them quickly, without sacrificing normal management controls.
As much testing of the urgent change as is possible should be carried out. Completely untested changes should not be implemented if it is at all avoidable. When changes go wrong, the cost is usually much greater than that incurred through testing. If an urgent change is carried out, and not all activities of the proper procedure have been taken care of, these activities should be planned and taken care of at the earliest opportunity. This will make sure that basic Risk Management considerations that are part of the Change Management procedure are given proper attention. E.g., if a CI has not been tested properly, the test should planned as soon as possible.

It may not be possible to update all Change Management records at the time when urgent actions are being completed (e.g. during overnight or weekend working). It is, however, essential that manual records are updated during such periods, and it is the responsibility of Change Management to ensure that all records are completed retrospectively, at the earliest possible opportunity. This helps to ensure valuable management and related information is not lost. An example could be the updating of an attribute defining 'success', 'failure' or perhaps 'partial failure' of a change. The updating should be carried out by the person responsible for applying the change, and should happen no later than the Post Implementation Review. Cooperation from the project team, Release Manager or Application Software Development Manager is expected.

7.4 Topics & theory 'Optimize'

7.4.1 Post-Implementation Review - PIR
Change Management should instigate follow-up actions to correct any problems or inefficiencies arising in the Change Management system itself as a result of ineffective changes. Change Management review may also show problems in other processes, such as Problem Management, in the reliability of system components, or in staff or user procedures and/or training.

Service Management should review the Change Management process periodically for efficiency and effectiveness. Such a review should be carried out shortly after the Change Management process is implemented, to ensure that the plans were carried out correctly and that the process is functioning as intended. Any problem should be tracked back to source and corrected as soon as possible.

Change Management must review all changes after a certain period has elapsed. How long this takes will depend on the priority and the category of the change. For example, urgent changes will be reviewed as soon as possible whereas minor changes can be reviewed at the next CAB meeting, or even on a longer term basis.

Change review has several objectives which may be related to with customer satisfaction or the effectiveness of the change process and/or procedures itself. Another objective, namely to determine whether the change has lead to the required results is shared with Problem Management. Many changes and releases implemented are instigated by Problem Management to resolve known errors in the infrastructure, or to implement fixes and workarounds to solve problem related incidents.

This specific type of review is what the PIR is all about. The objective of the PIR is to verify with all stakeholders whether the predefined result has been achieved. If the change had the goal of implementing a quick fix on a PC in order to stop certain incidents from occurring, the PIR may be as simple as spot-checking with the affected user. The PIR can also be an agenda entry for the change review meeting or even for a separate meeting to discuss the results of a Major Release.

For problem related changes the results of the review are crucial, because only after a positive review may the known error record be closed and, as a result of this, also the related problem and incident records. The review may also be a good indicator of the quality of the solutions proposed by Problem Management as part of the RFCs that are submitted to Change Management in order to resolve known errors or provide workarounds for problems and incidents.

7.4.2 Standard changes

Another way of improving the handling of changes is introducing the concept of standard changes. A standard change is a predefined change that:
- is relatively simple,
- causes limited risk,
- follows an established path,
- is processed frequently,
- and is accepted as being the default way of handling the requested modification of an infrastructure item.

While completely opposite to the secure and risk-avoiding nature of Change Management, speed is required to support the business processes. Creating standard changes improves the speed of handling this type of change: it doesn't require formal considerations in the change process, it doesn't require decisions by parties that have a meeting just once a week (CAB).

It also reduces the coordination resources that are spent on the change: the standard change can be handled by service desk staff or any other authorized staff (e.g. Operations) available.

And finally it improves the practical value of the service catalog by supporting a more differentiated service menu for the user. Standard changes like "Move a PC to another room", "Add a printer to a workstation", "Add 10MB to my mailbox storage capacity" are simple actions that may be requested by users, addressing the service desk directly. If standardized and covered by the SLA, having these actions in place as standard changes can make life much easier for users.

Standard changes:
- can be proposed by the CAB,
- can be authorized at user level beforehand,
- can be priced at default cost levels, which are agreed in the SLA.

7.5   Relationships

Problem Management
Change Management receives RFCs for the resolution of errors identified by Problem Management.
In turn, Change Management informs Problem Management of the identified errors that have been resolved through a specific change.

Configuration Management
Each change holds consequences for one or more CIs, and Configuration Management provides the relevant information.
Configuration Management is also responsible for helping to assess the consequences of a change on other related or dependent CIs.

By looking at the links between CIs, it is easy to establish which CIs are involved in a change. Even during the change period, Configuration Management must be kept informed of all the status changes being made to CIs.

Incident Management and Service Desk

Incident Management and the Service Desk are kept informed of all planned changes (FSC) and their related status (RFC).

Incident Management will issue an RFC when an incident requires a modification to the infrastructure. The RFC will be sent to the Change Management process.

Release Management

Change Management will send a release request to Release Management once the change has been constructed and tested and is ready to be implemented.

Release Management will keep the Change Management process informed of the Release Schedule.

Tactical Processes

Tactical Processes will require information about the RFC in order to analyze the impact from an Availability, Capacity, Continuity, Financial and Service Level Management aspect.

In return, the Tactical Processes will identify the impact from their specific area of expertise.

Project Management

Change Management has interaction with the discipline of project management (which is not an ITIL process). Change Management is responsible for coordinating the development, testing and implementing of the change. Project management can be made responsible for a specific phase of the change, e.g. the actual construction, tests or implementation.

7.6   Change Management tips & templates

This paragraph offers a series of tips and templates that can be used to support the Change Management process:
- Change roles
- Techniques for change impact analysis
- Request for Change (RFC) form
- Task list for deployment
- Change Calendar
- Metrics template

7.6.1   Change Management Roles and Responsibilities

Change Requestor

A Change Requestor is responsible for the initiation of a change and the registration and submittance of an RFC. After having identified the need for a change, the Change Requestor will generate an RFC in the Service Management tool, and will ensure that all relevant details for the change are complete and accurate. The Change Requestor is also responsible for providing the Change Coordinator with sufficient information in order to accept the RFC and have the change approved by the CAB. If the Change Coordinator decides to reject the RFC and the Change Requestor and Change Coordinator are unable to settle their differences, the Change Requestor can escalate the RFC to the higher management.

Change Coordinator

The Change Coordinator has 'end-to-end' responsibility for a change. After an RFC has been submitted by a Change Requestor, the Change Coordinator is responsible for accepting or rejecting the RFC. After rejecting an RFC, they are responsible for informing the Change Requestor of reasons for rejection. After accepting an RFC, they are responsible for providing information to the CAB members before a CAB meeting takes place. The Change Coordinator is also responsible for keeping all relevant parties and the CAB informed of the status and progress of the change. If the change is not completed in a timely manner, they should create a management by exception report. When the change has not been implemented successfully, it is the responsibility of the Change Coordinator to notify the CAB about the various solutions available to the Change Handler and/or Change Project Leader.

The Change Coordinator is also responsible for various administrative tasks: the closure of rejected RFCs at intake, and the closure of RFCs that have not been approved by the CAB. Furthermore, after implemented changes have been signed-off by all relevant parties, the RFC should be closed by the Coordinator.

Every region within a larger organization can appoint a local Coordinator; a global Change Coordinator will then coordinate all communications and inter-relations between the regions.

Change Project Leader

A Change Project Leader, if assigned, is responsible for managing the implementation of one or more change phases and will report to the Change Coordinator.

Change Handler

A Change Handler is responsible for the realization of specific activities in a change (e.g. plan, build, test, implement) and will report to the Project Leader or the Change Coordinator.

Change Reviewer

The role of Change Reviewer is to ensure that the change, as defined in the RFC database, is reviewed properly after successful implementation and sign-off of the Change Handler/Change Project Leader. The Change Reviewer is to verify whether the change has achieved its purpose after indication of the Change Coordinator that the change has been completed. Furthermore, the change should be accepted and signed-off by all relevant parties and this is also the responsibility of the Change Reviewer. As a result of the sign-off the change will be supported by Operations.

Change Advisory Board (CAB)

The CAB is responsible for the assessment and approval of all changes with the exception of standard changes. Final approval for implementation of all scheduled and maintenance change requests rests with the Change Manager; the CAB is the most important advisory council for the Change Manager. The CAB will be kept informed of the progress of all changes by the Change Coordinator and can propose standard changes.

Under normal conditions, CAB membership would be made up of:
- change Manager
- customer representatives
- user management
- user group representative team leads
- application developers/maintainers
- experts/technical consultants
- office services staff
- vendors (if involved - for instance in outsourcing situations).

Change Manager

The Change Manager is the person accountable for all activities and results of the Change Management process.

The accountability of a Change Manager is focused on:
- realizing the Key Performance Indicators (KPIs) for Change Management;
- ensuring the completeness and reliability of the RFC database;
- developing, maintaining, adjusting and documenting a clear and streamed Change Management process;
- integrating the Change Management process with other Service Management processes;
- ensuring all activities in the process are being done timely;
- functional managing the Change Management tools; and
- matching the RFC data model to the process and information needs.

Typical tasks of the Change Manager are:
- Ensuring that CAB meetings are held on a regular basis and arranging ad hoc CAB/EC meetings for all emergency changes.
- Issuing the agenda and distributing RFCs to CAB members in advance of meetings, to allow prior consideration.
- Documenting decisions made during the CAB meeting and distributing information about plans/schedules and resource allocation.
- Inviting additional individuals to the CAB meeting where necessary for specific change requests.
- Monitoring the execution of the Change Management process and taking timely corrective action.
- Evaluating the process (including reporting) and tools in regular meetings with team leaders and other process managers.
- Initiating required changes and extensions to the datamodel by meeting regularly with technical developers and supporters of the RFC database.
- Ensuring timely reporting to management.

To realize such responsibilities and accountabilities the Change Manager is authorized to direct team leaders to execute the required activities to ensure a correct and timely Change Management process.

7.6.2 Techniques for change impact analysis

There are many tools and techniques that you can use to help you evaluate the positive and negative aspects of making changes. This section introduces two approaches:
1. The basics of **SWOT Analysis**
2. The basics of **Risk Analysis and Risk Management**

Much of what is described below, applies only to changes which need to be referred to the CAB – ie the big ones. However, the principles still apply to any change, not matter how small it may be.

SWOT Analysis

SWOT (Strengths, Weaknesses, Opportunities, Threats) will help you to highlight the key issues associated with a change.
The technique attempts to answer two basic questions:
1. What is the current position of this application, system, product, service or supplier - its strengths and weaknesses?
2. What changes could make it more (or less) effective - the opportunities and threats?

The following Service Desk example illustrates SWOT from two viewpoints:
- **Internal analysis** - examine the internal operation and characteristics of the Service Desk so that you identify its existing strengths and weaknesses.
- **External analysis** - search to determine the potential and longer term opportunities and threats posed from outside the Service Desk (or the business) – the external environment.

This following example should be sufficiently self-explanatory and help you understand the key principles:

Strength	Weakness
We are well known in the organization and have an excellent reputation; this means that...	We have not been benchmarked for two years; this means that....
We provide consistent products and help users with their current requirements; this means that........	Governance, new applications and services and recent policy changes particularly regarding service X are causing us resourcing and other difficulties; this means that......
We are "working towards" ISO20000 accreditation; this means that....	We have lost half our staff in the last three months; this means that...
Opportunity	**Threat**
Company Z is in acquisition talks with us. There is also talk of merger with other departments; this means that...	Company Z is in acquisition talks with us. There is also talk of merger with other departments; this means that.....

Table 7.1 SWOT Analysis Example

The phrase 'this means that' should help to:
1. identify the actions required to reduce the immediate weaknesses and the longer term threats;
2. identify the actions required to increase the immediate strengths and build on the longer term opportunities.

SWOT analysis is used to help focus on the big picture associated with changes whilst Risk Management can help to focus on the details of the changes, specifically the probability and impact of making changes to services and applications running on the live infrastructure.

Risk Analysis and Risk Management

The purpose of Risk Analysis and Risk Management is to improve the chances of making the change a success by:

1. recognizing the risks;
2. analyzing the impact and probability of each risk, this involves the identification and definition of risks, plus the evaluation of impact and consequent actions;
3. taking actions to minimize the risks; this is Risk Management. It covers the activities involved in planning, monitoring and controlling the actions that will address the weaknesses and threats identified during the SWOT and Risk Analysis processes, thereby helping to make the change a success with few back-outs.

> *What Is a Risk?*
> *A risk is any possible event that may prevent the change from being successful. Risk is subjective and its identification depends on the experience, perception and attitude of the "risk assessor".*

Risk Management is an integral part of Change Management. If you wish to manage changes properly you will need to adopt Risk Management methods.

The main objective of the Risk Management process is to ensure that risks have been identified, impacts assessed and mitigation tasks described and allocated; these should help reduce or eliminate these risks.

Each change has at least one associated risk. The Change Manager will work with key stakeholders (typically members of the CAB) to identify:

- The **probability** of the risk occurring. This is an evaluated likelihood of a particular outcome actually happening.
- The **impact** of the risk. This is the evaluated effect or result of a particular outcome actually happening. Impact may be affected by:
  - dependencies, time, cost, quality
  - scope, urgency, benefit
  - people / resources or
  - other factors.

You may be able to evaluate risks in numerical terms – these are often associated with capacity, availability or money. Other risks, such as those related to changes to an application, may affect job roles, processes or other intangible aspects that can only be evaluated subjectively.

To evaluate the impact of the change (positive as well as negative) many people use a simple framework for categorizing risks, for example high, medium and low - or 3/2/1. The Change Manager will also consider when the risk is likely to occur - next day or next year. By doing so, people focus on those risks that are about to happen - the 'risk proximity'.

Much of this will be documented in the Change Log - see the example a few pages onwards.

Identify suitable responses and actions to the risk

The actions break into broadly five types (see table 7.2).

Prevention	Terminate the risk – by doing things differently and thus removing the risk, where it is feasible to do so. Countermeasures are put in place that either stop the threat or problem from occurring or prevent it having any impact on the project or business
Reduction	Treat the risk – take action to control it in some way where the actions either reduce the likelihood of the risk developing or limit the impact on the live systems or services to acceptable levels
Transference	This is a specialist form of risk reduction where the management of the risk is passed to a third party via, for instance, an insurance policy or penalty clause, such that the impact of the risk is no longer an issue for the health of the project. Not all risks can be transferred in this way.
Acceptance	Tolerate the risk – perhaps because nothing can be done at a reasonable cost to mitigate it or the likelihood and impact of the risk occurring are at an acceptable level
Contingency	These are actions planned and organized to come into force as and when the risk occurs

Table 7.2   Five types of actions to risks

Any risk could have appropriate actions in any or all of these categories. There may be no cost-effective actions available to deal with a risk, in which case the risk must be accepted or the justification for the change revisited (to review whether the change is too risky). This could result in rejection of the change request.

The results of the risk evaluation activities are documented in the Request For Change (Risk) - see the example a few pages onwards.

Select Options and Actions

The risk response should involve identifying and evaluating a range of options for treating risks and preparing and implementing Risk Management plans.

Selection of the risk actions to take is a balance between a number of things. For each possible action it is, first, a question of balancing the cost of taking that action against the likelihood and impact of allowing the risk to occur.

There may be several possible risk actions, each with different effects. The choice may be one of these options or a combination of two or more actions. You will need to consider the impact of (a) the risk occurring and (b) the risk action on:
• The Forward Schedule of Changes - see the example a few pages onwards.
• Resource, Team, Project, Build, Test, Release Plans.
• The business, programme, service management needs.
• Other parts of the infrastructure.

The actions and options chosen may depend on the appetite for risk –the 'risk tolerance'.

Risk Management

Plan and Resource

Having made the selection, the implementation of the selected actions will need planning and resourcing (see Change Management authorisation and approval). It is likely to include:
- Planning countermeasure actions itemized during the risk evaluation activities.
- Resourcing.

Monitor and Report

There must be mechanisms in place for monitoring and reporting on the actions selected to address risks. Change Management will need to ensure that;
- Execution of the planned actions is having the desired effect.
- The overall management of change impact and risk is being applied effectively.

Risk profile

This is a simple mechanism to increase visibility of risks and assist management decision making. It is a graphical representation of information normally found in existing Risk Logs.

Any risk shown above and right of the 'risk tolerance line' (the thick black line) should be referred upwards.

As risks are reviewed, any changes to their impact or probability which cause them to move above and to the right of the 'risk tolerance line' need to be considered carefully and referred to the CAB or above for agreements on actions to be taken.

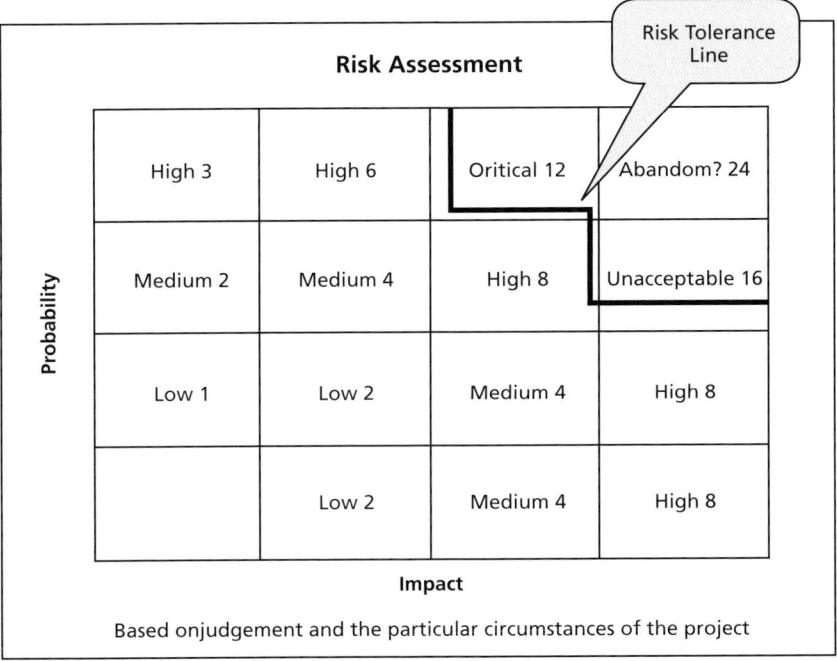

Figure 7.2   Risk profile

7.6.3 Relationship Change Management - Project Management

Summary of the Change Management process

The mandate of the production Change Management process is to protect the integrity of the production environment, and ensure that any changes introduced are planned and executed to a quality standard that minimizes the possibility of negative impact.

The Change Advisory Board (CAB) is a representative group, which ensures that all significant changes to the environment within its scope are adequately assessed for impact and resource requirements. The CAB will evaluate all submitted Requests for Change (RFC) on a weekly basis. A sub-set of the CAB (CAB/EC) will be called upon, on an exception basis, to evaluate urgent RFCs.

The CAB will review all RFCs, including IT initiated changes, against the business objectives. The CAB will also impartially assess the overall impact of the RFC on other projects within the production environment, based on the business and technical impact assessment.

Depending on the classification (minor, significant or major) of the change, the CAB will then either approve or disapprove the RFC or make a recommendation to the properly authorized person. Regardless of the decision, the Change Manager will convey the results to the Change Initiator. A right of appeal against a CAB rejection exists via normal management channels.

Responsibilities of the Project Manager

As a Project Manager, you must:
- be aware of the Change Management process;
- understand its requirements and communicate them to your project team;
- understand the timelines required by the process and integrate them into your project plan;
- understand the required documentation and ensure that it is completed on a timely basis and is accurate and understandable;
- submit all RFCs to the Change Manager for completeness check and initial logging/inclusion on the next available CAB agenda;
- advise the Change Manager of any revisions to RFCs that you have initiated;
- ensure revisions include timing, content, resources required, etc;
- integrate the conclusions of CAB into your project plan.

The Relationship between Change Management and Project Change Control

All projects are composed of the following activities, managed via a project plan and Project Manager. The diagram in Figure 7.3 lists the standard phases in the life cycle of a Prince2® project, and the relationships between the activities/phases.

All project management methodologies require that other management tools be applied to each activity to ensure that the final deliverables meet the necessary standards. Project Change Management (Change Control) is an activity that is designed to manage:
- potential Impacts on Project Deliverables created by changes in the Environment;
- change to Project Deliverables caused by changes in the Project Mandate;

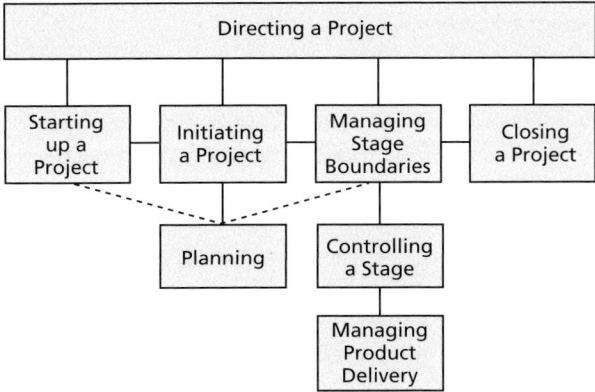

Figure 7.3   Phases in Prince2® project life cycle

- potential Impacts on Project Deliverables created by changes within the Structure of the Project.

Figure 7.4 is one of many tools used to navigate the project to a successful completion.

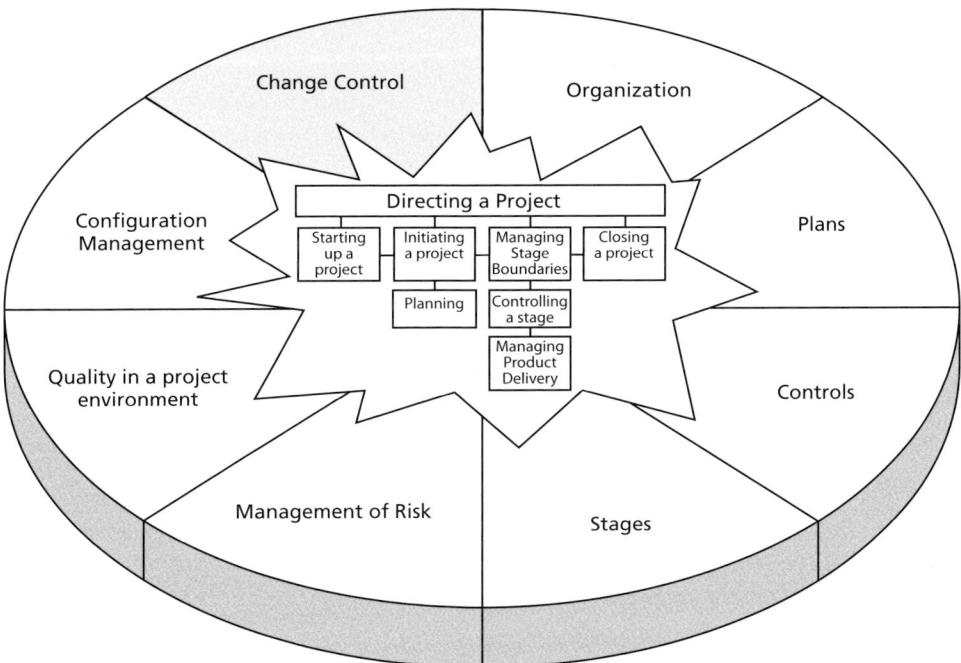

Figure 7.4   Project diagram

While Project Change Management may include Elements of the Production Change Management Process (i.e. Impact Analysis, Request for Change, etc) it is not a replacement for the Production Change Management Process. From a project point of view, the scope of the Cluster Process is far more focused on the management of the IT infrastructure, not on any other project related issues.

Project Change Management should be structured to integrate with the Cluster Process where necessary. Throughout the life of the project there will be infrastructure changes that will have to adhere to the Cluster Process. Examples of these include:

- **Project Initiation** – assigning Desktop resources/access to team members
- **Project Scope** – defining what access is necessary at what phase
- **Building Deliverables** – CAB will have to authorize the release of RFCs to development, sourcing, vendors, etc.
- **Migration to Production** – the Change Management process ensures that a clean transition to production is planned and executed.
- **Project Wind Up** – RFCs will be necessary to de-commission any equipment and wind up the resources allocated to the team.

Remember: The Production Change Management process does not replace Project Change Management, nor does it relieve the project manager of that responsibility.

Key Facts to Remember

IT Project initiation – There should be no IT project initiated outside of the Change Management process: all IT projects should be tied to an existing traceable RFC number. Even IT feasibility studies should go through the Change Management process and receive a mandate from the CAB.

CAB meets on a Scheduled basis – Initial submissions to CAB must be given to the Change Manager by the defined deadline. The Change Manager will review each proposed RFC for completeness before it is accepted and logged. CAB will review this RFC and make its recommendations within the times of acceptance as defined by by the Change Manager.

Work time to Build the Change – In the event that the CAB approves your change and releases it for creation, resources must be available to do the work and create the deliverables. CAB approval does not create a budget for the work to be done, the RFC should indicate that you have resources allocated and funded to do any project specific work. Work that falls under general application/infrastructure support will be prioritized by the CAB in relation to other demands on those resources.

Testing Cycles – The CAB does not manage the testing cycles required to produce a finished change, it is the responsibility of the Project Manager appointed to that phase. You must allow time and resources in your project plan to meet the testing standards the CAB defines. The CAB will request a final sign-off from all stakeholders in the change to indicate that all required testing, documentation, business support, functionality, etc, has been delivered.

Deployment – When integrating final deployment of changes into your project plan, be sure to consult both the Change Manager, the Release Manager, and the Forward Schedule of Changes (approved by the CAB). Available deployment windows (in the Change Calendar) are very limited at this time, and they fill up quickly. Do not assume that the date which has been initially requested will be available, nor that the initial date received from the Change Manager will be the final date. Be sure to check back with the Change Manager on a regular basis for status updates.

Project Delays – If any of the elements of the project are delayed and the delays will impact submitted changes, be sure to advise Change Management immediately. Dependencies between RFCs can often have impact far beyond any obvious delays

7.6.4 Request for Change form

1.0 Change Summary:			
1.1 Change Title:			
1.2 Project Title (if any):			
1.3 Submitted by:		1.5 Change Owner:	
1.4 Date Submitted		1.6 Related RFCs	
	Requested:	Approved:	
1.7 Type:			
1.8 Deployment Date/Time:			
1.9 Estimated Duration:			
1.10 Urgency:			
1.11 Impact:			
1.12 Risk:			
2.0 What is the Purpose of the Change?			
2.1 Describe the Issue/Concept:			
2.2 Incident References:		2.3 Problem References:	
3.0 Review of Alternative Solutions and Recommendation			
3.1 Describe the Alternative Solutions Available:			
3.2 Recommended Solution and Justification:			
3.3 Benefits / Impact to the Business:			
3.4 Benefits / Impact to IT:			
4.0 How will we implement this change?			
4.1 High Level Description:			

table continues on the next page

4.2 Detailed Task List:		
4.3 List of Configuration Items Affected:		
5.0 Have we thought of everything?		
5.1	Implementation Plan	
5.2	Test Plan	
5.3	Back out Plan	
5.4	User Involvement	
5.5	Communication (Users, Management, Help Desk)	
5.6	Security	
5.7	Resources (Skills, Availability)	
5.8	Environment (Heat, Fire, Power, Access, Space)	
5.9	Technical Documentation (Physical/Logical Architecture)	
5.10	Written Support Procedures	
5.11	Cost Estimates	
6.0 What are the impacts & risks?		
√ if Yes	**6.1 : Potential Impact areas**	**6.2 Mitigating Action:**
	Impacts to 3rd party information exchanges	
	Performance and Capacity potential impacts (servers, network, bandwidth, licences)	
	Impacts to server hardware and hardware configuration requirements	
	Application interfaces impacted	
	Changes to transaction and data update frequency and volumes	
	Changes to shared functions	
	Impacts to access, security, accounts	
	Changes to escalation and on call support procedures	
	Design documentation impacts	
	Operation procedures documentation impacts	
	User documentation impacts	
	Technical information documentation impacts	
	Technology Standards Apply/Known	
	Impacts to scripts and batch jobs	
	Changes to database (structure, formats, rules)	
	Impacts due to name or naming convention changes	
	Impacts to Existing incident Resolutions	
	Impacts to Reporting systems and applications	
	Impacts to Internet/E-commerce systems and applications	
	Impacts to Service Desk and support training and procedures (workarounds, recovery procedures, support procedures, problem determination and diagnosis procedures)	

table continues on the next page

	Impacts to Desktop image, software and configuration requirements			
	Impacts to System Reporting requirements			
	Impact to disaster recovery documentation and procedures			
	Risks of negative impacts to Daily operations			
	Impacts to development tool requirements			
	Major impacts to development and testing environments			
	Business Impacts			
	Risks of negative impacts to business			
	Significant User Desktop Environment Changes?			
	Policy Decisions Impacted?			
	Training Plan Necessary?			
	Knowledge Transfer Plan? (for new Functionality)			
	Changes to Existing Work Arounds?			
	Meets Business Requirements?			

7.0 Approval to Build

Name	Role	Signature	Date

8.0 Approval to Deploy

Name	Role	Signature	Date

9.0 Deployment Success/Failure

9.1 Was the Change Successfully Deployed?

Name	Role	Signature	Date

7.6.5   Task list for deployment of RFC

Item	Who	Action Item	Status	Start time	End Time	Notes
Task list for deployment of RFC Please Note: All times are subject to change due						For promotion status updates, please dial
		Prior to Deployment Date				
		Actions on Deployment Day				
		Actions After Deployment Day				
		Other Subsequent Events				

7.6.6 Change Calendar

2005 Change Schedule

January

Sun	Mon	Tue	Wed	Thu	Fri	Sat
						1
2	C U K 3	M 4	M 5	M 6	M 7	M 8
M 9	M 10	11	12	13	14	15
16	17			20	21	22
23	24	X 25	P 26	P 27	P 28	29
30	P 31					

February

Sun	Mon	Tue	Wed	Thu	Fri	Sat
		M 1	M 2	M 3	M 4	M 5
6	M 7	B 8	M 9	B 10	M 11	M 12
13	M 14	M 15	16		18	19
20	C U 21	22	23	24	X 25	P 26
P 27	P 28					

March

Sun	Mon	Tue	Wed	Thu	Fri	Sat
		M 1	M 2	M 3	M 4	M 5
6	7	M 8	M 9	M 10	M 11	12
13	14	15	16		18	19
20	21	22	23	24	C U 25	26
27	C K 28	P 29	P 30	P 31		

April

Sun	Mon	Tue	Wed	Thu	Fri	Sat
					M 1	M 2
M 3	M 4	M 5	M 6	M 7	M 8	9
10	11	12	13	14	15	16
17	18		20	21	22	23
24	X 25	B P 26	P 27	P 28	P 29	30

May

Sun	Mon	Tue	Wed	Thu	Fri	Sat
1	M 2	M 3	M 4	M 5	M 6	M 7
8	M 9	M 10	11	12	13	14
15	16	17			C K 20	E 21
22	C K 23	24	X 25	P 26	U P K 27	28
29	U P 30	P 31				

June

Sun	Mon	Tue	Wed	Thu	Fri	Sat
			M 1	M 2	M 3	M 4
5	M 6	7	M 8	M 9	M 10	11
12	13	14	15	16		18
19	20	21	22	23	X 24	25
26	P 27	P 28	P 29	P 30		

July

Sun	Mon	Tue	Wed	Thu	Fri	Sat
					C M U K 1	M 2
M 3	U M 4	M 5	M 6	M 7	C K 8	9
10	11	B 12	B 13	B 14	15	16
17	18		20	21	22	23
24	X 25	P 26	P 27	P 28	C P K 29	30
31						

August

Sun	Mon	Tue	Wed	Thu	Fri	Sat
	C U K 1	M 2	M 3	M 4	M 5	M 6
7	M 8	M 9	M 10	11	12	13
14	15	16		19	20
21	22	23	24	X 25	P 26	27
28	P 29	P 30	P 31			

September

Sun	Mon	Tue	Wed	Thu	Fri	Sat
				M 1	C U K 2	M 3
4	C U 5	M 6	M 7	M 8	M 9	M 10
M 11	M 12	13	14	15	16	17
18	19	20	21	22	23	24
25	X 26	P 27	P 28	P 29	P 30	

October

Sun	Mon	Tue	Wed	Thu	Fri	Sat
						M 1
M 2	M 3	M 4	M 5	M 6	7	8
9	C U K 10	11	B 12	B 13	14	15
16	17		20	21	22
23	24	X 25	P 26	P 27	P 28	29
30	P 31					

November

Sun	Mon	Tue	Wed	Thu	Fri	Sat
		M 1	M 2	M 3	M 4	M 5
6	7	M 8	M 9	C 10	C K 11	12
13	14	15	16		18	19
20	21	22	23	U 24	X U 25	P 26
27	P 28	P 29	P 30			

December

Sun	Mon	Tue	Wed	Thu	Fri	Sat
			M 1	M 2	M 3
4	B M 5	B M 6	M 7	M 8	M 9	M 10
11	12	13	14	15	16	17
18	19		20	21	22	X U 23	24
25	C U 26	C K 27	P 28	P 29	P 30	P 31

Legend:

- B — Board Meeting
- X — EURO Cheque Exchange
- Euro Cheque Exchange Preparation
- E — US Cheque Exchange
- US Cheque Exchange Preparation
- EURO & US Cheque Exchange Preparation
- Board Meeting Preparation
- C — Cardigan Office Closed
- U — Denver Office Closed
- K — Mktg Traders Working on US Office Holidays
- M — Corp Acctg Month-end Processing
- P — Prod Acctg Month-end Processing
- Emergency Change Only
- No outages to be scheduled
- Low Impact Changes Only
- All changes, Subject to Approval

No changes during Business hours
(8:00 AM - 5:00 PM Local)

7.6.7. Metrics template sample

Part 1 - DESCRIPTION	
Process or Function Name:	
Metrics Name:	
Definition and Calculation:	
Frequency:	Yearly/Quarterly/Monthly
Break down:	
Origin:	
Part 2 - COMPARISON	
With an objective?	
With a margin or a standard?	
Relating to time?	
With others?	
Part 3 - PRESENTATION	
Part 4 – INTERPRETATION and POSSIBLE ACTIONS	
Interpretation:	
Possible actions:	

Metrics Author:
Create Date:
Last Amended by:
Last Amendment Date:
Status:
Version:

7.7   Knowledge test questions

Question 1
According to the scope of the proposed change, Requests for Change will be processed following predefined change models, e.g. for standard, minor, substantial and major changes. How are these change models to be prepared and authorized?
A.   Change models are defined by Change Management and authorized by the CAB
B.   Change models are defined by support staff and authorized by the Change Manager
C.   Change models are defined by Change Management and authorized by the organization

Question 2
The project manager responsible for implementing the XYZ application has ordered the roll-out of the client software. His project plan has been approved by the CAB at the start of the project.
Can the roll-out be part of the next release without a Request for Change?
A.   No. The project manager lacks the authority to request the implementation and a Request for Change is needed from the organization's management to ensure the implementation is properly authorized.

B. No. The roll-out of the client software is a change and needs to be coordinated via Change Management. All Change Management procedures apply, including the need for a Request for Change.

C. Yes. The project manager is responsible for the implementation. The project manager only needs to inform Change Management of the planning of upcoming changes.

D. Yes. The project plan was, in fact, a Request for Change and the CAB has already agreed.

Question 3
What is the difference between the Forward Schedule of Changes (FSC) and the Projected Service Availability (PSA)?

A. The FSC is based on the PSA and not the other way around.

B. The FSC holds information on availability of CIs, the PSA does not.

C. The PSA is based on the FSC and not the other way around.

D. The PSA needs to be agreed with the customer, the FSC does not.

7.8 Practical assignments

7.8.1 Planning Change Management activities

Description
Aligning the Change Management Plan with the business planning cycle.

Goals
Describe the business planning cycle:
1. Define the Change Management deliverables that are needed as input of the business planning cycle.
2. Describe the outputs of the business planning cycle that are needed as input for the Change Management Plan.

Implementation
One may use the planning and budgeting cycle of the own organization. The Change Management Plan for this organization is not needed; an outline of such a Change Management Plan is part of the assignment.

It is important in this assignment is to consider how the business planning cycle will affect the Change Management Plan.

Assessment criteria during the process
1. Has collected and used all relevant information on the business planning cycle.
2. Has collected and used all relevant documentation on the Change Management Plan (including both Managing and Organizing activities).
3. Use of communication skills collecting the information.
4. Proper organization off information.

Assessment criteria for the result
1. Outline of the business planning cycle.
2. Outline of the Change Management Plan.
3. Description of inputs and outputs to and from the business planning cycle and the Change Management Plan.

7.8.2 Change Management and Release Schedule

Description
Convincing an audience of the effectiveness of a Release Schedule.

Goals
- Prepare a proposal for the introduction of a Release Schedule.
- Prepare a presentation to a meeting of the Release & Control team staff.
- Discuss the advantages and disadvantages for Change Management of the introduction of the Release Schedule.

8 Certification in Release & Control

8.1 Introduction

Internationally recognized qualifications for professionals in IT Service Management (ITSM) are of increasing importance to organizations and to individual professionals. Many organizations require their staff both to speak a common language and to have common qualifications, regardless of where the individuals may reside or where the qualification is gained.
Individual professionals want to improve their career opportunities, and to provide evidence of their proficiency in the common language and of their skills in IT Service Management.

Optimizing professionalism is an important element of successful IT Service improvement programs, and staff commitment for such programs can be boosted by challenging and rewarding employees with internationally recognized certifications.

While ITIL® provides the common language in IT Service Management, the international IT Service Management qualifications based on the ITIL approach provide recognized evidence of professionalism in IT Service Management.

The ITSM qualification program driven by EXIN and ISEB is the only training and qualification program leading to official certificates in IT Service Management that are relevant in practice. The development of the qualification program by EXIN and ISEB was endorsed by OGC and itSMF International.

The qualification program aims at certifying the understanding, skills and capabilities of individuals, in the complex and necessary IT Service Management processes. These qualifications and the training and examinations related to these qualifications are available worldwide, and continue to evolve to meet market needs and the developments in IT Service Management.

Internationally recognized certification is one of the important factors in the success of ITIL as a standard. For the users, particularly in organizations that operate internationally, it is of vital importance that the 'common language' that ITIL claims to provide is really used in a consistent way from Sydney to Stockholm and from Cincinnati to Kuala Lumpur. In that regard, the ITSM certificates function as a worldwide 'golden standard'.

8.1.1 Examination bodies

Qualifications are available only from the official Examination Institutes (EI). These are organizations that have a proven track record in the provision of examinations and have an excellent reputation. The Examination Institutes cooperate with experts in the field to ensure their processes and procedures the constant quality and integrity of the examinations. The IT Service Management examinations are based on the Best Practice documented in the ITIL books and attuned to the latest developments in the field of IT Service Management.

The EI is responsible for generating exam questions based on the common 'syllabuses'. This allows scope for questions/exams to be developed in the local language and also allows cultural differences and various business perspectives to be accounted for, while retaining the commonality and standard of the resulting qualification.

In order to facilitate the global provision of examinations, an Examination Institute can appoint Examination Agents (EA) to act on their behalf. Such an Agent will have a proven track record in the provision of examinations and will be accredited by the EI, according the EI's rules and regulations.

The venue for the examination is provided either by an Examination Institute, an Examination Agent or an Examination Center authorized by one of the accredited Examination Institutes. The Authorized Examination Center will ensure that the examination is set and supervised according to the rules and regulations of the Examination Institute.

Details about Examination Agents and Examination Centers can be obtained via the two accredited Examination Institutes, EXIN and ISEB.

8.1.2 Accredited Course Providers

The quality of an ITSM course depends on many factors, including the quality of the tutors, planning of the course, the suitability of the venue, the consistency of the course materials with the ITIL books, the experience of the attendees, the use of practice oriented examples, assignments and the opportunities for group discussions.

The Examination Institutes cooperate closely with their accredited training organizations to monitor the quality of the ITSM training provided and to implement improvements where necessary.
The accredited training providers are supplied with the latest updates on the syllabus and sample papers for the official ITSM examinations.

Most of the recognized qualifications require the candidate to attend a training course offered by an Accredited Course Provider. Course Providers are accredited by an Examination Institute according to the EI's rules and regulations.
The ITSM Certification program also aids organizations and individuals in the evaluation of the training providers and the course materials.

The common framework of accreditation rules of the official Examination Institutes ensure:
• the quality of the organization of training by the accredited course provider;
• the knowledge, understanding and experience of the trainers of the course provider, both in IT Service Management and in education;
• the quality of the training materials used;
• agreement on the course content with the requirements for the examinations in the ITSM qualification program.

The Examination Institutes have published the requirements for accredited course providers on their websites.

To ensure the impartiality of the Examination Institutes in the accreditation of course providers and the marking of the examinations, the Examination Institutes do not provide IT Service Management training and operate independently from the commercial interests of the course providers.

8.1.3 Qualification Program

The international ITSM Certification Program currently consists of three kinds of certificates:
- the ITSM Foundation Certificate in IT Service Management
- the ITSM Practitioner Certificates in IT Service Management
- the ITSM Manager's Certificate in IT Service Management

Figure 8.1 Certificates in IT Service Management

The Foundation Certificate is designed to provide a foundation level of knowledge in IT Service Management. It is aimed at all personnel who wish to become familiar with the best practices for IT Service Management, as defined in the IT Infrastructure Library (ITIL) guidelines. In particular, it enables people to understand the terminology used within the ITIL approach.

The Practitioner Certificates are aimed at those who take part within their organization in managing, organizing and optimizing specific processes within the IT Service Management discipline, and performing the activities that belong to those processes. The Examination Institutes provide Practitioner certification for several IT Service Management processes, or clusters of processes, like the Practitioner Release & Control (Release Management, Change Management and Configuration Management), the Practitioner Support & Restore (Incident Management, Problem Management and and Service Desk), the Practitioner Agree & Define (Service Level Management and Financial Management for IT Services) and in the near future the Practitioner Plan & Improve (Capacity Management, Availibility Management and IT Service Continuity Management). An accredited training course for the Practitioner Certificates will not only provide the background knowledge and understanding of the relevant IT Service Management processes, but also offer the opportunity to develop practical skills during assignments.

While the Foundation Certificate is primarily focused on understanding the terminology and the Practitioner Certificates on the processes in a specific area, the *Manager's Certificate* is aimed at those who need to demonstrate a capability of managing ITIL-based solutions across the breadth of the Service Management subjects. An accredited training course for the Manager's Certificate will also provide opportunity to develop managerial skills in a series of case study related assignments.

Each Examination Institute publishes the syllabus for each examination it offers, based on the **agreed common syllabus**. Examination Institutes, Examination Agents and Accredited Course Providers will publish their own rules and regulations governing the operation of their part of the program, e.g. fees, payment schedules, lead times for exams, appeals, etc. They must conform to general principles.

It has been a well-known tradition for years that passing an ITSM-exam not only results in a certificate, but is also accompanied by a pin, a green one for passing the ITSM Foundation examination, a blue one for ITSM Practitioner and a red one for ITSM Manager.

Figure 8.2   ITSM Pin

8.1.4   Benefits of the ITSM certification program

Earning an independent certificate represents solid evidence of your successful completion of the course requirements. It illustrates your dedication to becoming more competent and valuable to your organization and the customers you serve.

Benefits for the participants

Getting certified helps you to:
- strengthen your skills and improve your job performance;
- update your knowledge in the field of your choice;
- boost your value to your employer;
- qualify for jobs that require specialized knowledge;
- launch a fulfilling new career;
- receive recognition from the industry and your peers;
- stay competitive.

Benefits to the business

Getting certified also provides benefits to your company's business:
- better use of human resources;
- proven quality of your IT staff;
- possibilities to distinguish who is skilled for the job;
- specific knowledge and skills needed to perform an IT job successfully;
- incentives, rewards and challenges for employees.

The certification program has helped companies to identify the need for training of IT Service Management staff. Any organization that decides to really use the ITIL framework to improve IT services needs to be conscious that a lot of staff will be involved one way or another. Most of them probably do not need to be experts, but some fluency in the common language, i.e. ITIL, is crucial.

Training in the Foundations of IT Service Management will provide the attendees with an overview of IT Service Management, the main processes and their relationships. It often also helps to pave the way for the changes in attitude, culture and procedures necessary to improve customer focus and professional IT service delivery. The Foundation Certificate in IT Service Management is both a reward for the attendees of such training and a way of measuring the progress of ITIL knowledge and awareness in your organization. The ITSM Certification program will also aid in the evaluation of the training providers and the course materials.

To develop and implement your company's plans for improving IT Service Management processes, you should rely on professionals with a proven record of achievements in this area. The cornerstone of such a profile will be the Manager's Certificate in IT Service Management. Once the processes have been brought to a degree of maturity where they can be managed and controlled, you will need professionals with skills in the various process areas. The ITSM certification program provides a certification for these types of professionals, the Practitioner Certificate in IT Service Management.

Availability

The Foundation examinations are available in Dutch, English, French, Spanish (Latin American), Spanish (European), German, Portuguese, Chinese, Japanese, Russian, Arabic, Italian, Swedish, Korean. The combined Practitioner examinations (clusters) are available in English, German, Dutch, French, Spanish and Japanese. The Service Manager examinations are available in English, German, Russian, Dutch, French, Spanish and Japanese. Details of the availability of accredited training and examinations can be obtained from the Examination Institutes.

8.1.5 Requirements for the Practitioner Certificate Release & Control

The Practitioner Certificate in IT Service Management: Release & Control is aimed at those who take part within their organization in managing, organizing and optimizing the IT Service Management processes Release Management, Change Management and Configuration Management, and performing the activities that belong to those processes. The Examination Institutes provide Practitioner certification for several IT Service Management processes, or clusters of processes, like the Practitioner Release & Control (Release Management, Change Management and Configuration Management), the Practitioner Support & Restore (Incident Management, Problem Management and Service Desk), the Practitioner Agree & Define (Service Level Management and Financial Management for IT Services and in the near future the Practitioner Plan & Improve (Capacity Management, Availability Management and IT Service Continuity Management). An accredited training course for the Practitioner Certificates will not only provide the background knowledge and understanding of the relevant IT Service Management processes, but also offer the opportunity to develop practical skills during assignments.

The requirements for the Practitioner Certificate Release & Control are:
• The ITSM Foundation Certificate in IT Service Management.
• Attending an accredited Practitioner Release & Control training.
• Successfully completing three practical assignments:
    – Configuration Management Assignment
    – Change Management Assignment
    – Release Management Assignment
• Passing the ITSM Practitioner Release & Control exam.

In the Practitioner Certificate in IT Service Management Release and Control examination the following subjects are covered:
• Managing the Release & Control processes
• Organizing the Release & Control processes
• Optimizing the Release & Control processes

Knowledge and skills in these areas will be tested in the examination. In particular:
• Managing:
    – plan the key activities for the Change Management, Release Management and Configuration Management processes;
    – plan the exchange of appropriate information relevant to managing the Release & Control processes;
    – initiate actions to ensure the key activities in the Release & Control processes meet the objectives set;
    – report on the effectiveness and efficiency of the activities in the Release & Control processes.

- Organizing:
  - organize the exchange of appropriate information with other processes;
  - provide Change, Release and Configuration Management information to other IT Service Management processes, users and suppliers;
  - maintain the procedures of the Release & Control processes;
  - maintain the baselines of configurations and the status information of Configuration Items;
  - provide instructions for designing, building and configuring releases;
  - advise on the back-out and test plans for changes and releases;
  - plan the implementation of releases;
  - monitor the logistics (storage, transport, deployment and/or delivery, implementation) for releases (whether purchased or developed internally);
  - coordinate and monitor changes (including preparing and taking part in Change Advisory Board meetings).
- Optimizing:
  - monitor and optimize the Release & Control processes;
  - propose improvements, based on results of monitoring and/or reviews;
  - plan and conduct change, release and configuration audits.

In the **practical assignments** the participant is given the opportunity to demonstrate the practical skills required for a Practitioner in Release & Control and to receive feedback and guidance from a professional coach (often the trainer of the accredited Practitioner course).

In each assignment at least two of the three main tasks (manage, organize and optimize) will occur. At least two out of these three assignments will cover tasks in the field of organizing a process. Each of the three processes, Release Management, Change Management and Configuration Management will be the main focus of one of the assignments, but the assignments typically cover areas of interaction between these processes.
The assignments are chosen by the coach/trainer as part of the accredited training course and are based on the guidelines from the exam institute.
Examples of such assignments are:
- reviewing Configuration Management reports;
- optimizing a change procedure;
- planning and implementing a release.

Assignments should either be fulfilled by real practice (i.e. in the working environment) or by a realistic simulation of such an environment. Each assignment will take approximately 18 hours (including preparation during the training).
The skills to be judged may vary, depending on the nature of the assignment set by the training organization, but in general should involve elements of:
1. creativity;
2. analytical thinking;
3. oral communication skills;
4. writing skills;
5. Release & Control skills.

The result of each assignment will be assessed based on:
• usefulness and applicability in practice;
• meeting the expectation of the (client) organization;
• showing application of best practice.

After successful fulfillment of all three practical assignments, the course provider reports to the Exam Institute regarding the results. The Exam Institute needs such a statement on completion of your practical assignments in advance of your registration for the exam.

EXIN Syllabus and services
The Syllabus (Exam Requirement) of the Foundation Certificate in IT Service Management exam is available through www.exin-exams.com. The exam and the requirements are available in 14 languages. The exams are also available through Prometric (www.prometric.com) and VUE (www.vue.com) in English and Japanese.

ISEB Syllabus and services
The Syllabus of the Foundation Certificate in IT Service Management exam is available through www.bcs.org/iseb. The exam and the requirements are available in English. The exams are also available through Prometric (www.prometric.com) in English.

8.2   Rules and regulations

8.2.1   Prerequisites
• The ITSM Foundation Certificate.
• Before taking the Practitioner examination the candidate must have attended accredited training and successfully completed the practical assignments.

The ITSM Foundation Certificate is a prerequisite for attending an accredited training course.

8.2.2   Exam format
The exam consists of a two hour, closed-book, 40 question, multiple-choice paper.
For each question, several options are given (with a maximum of four). The candidate must select the correct answer. One mark is awarded for a correct answer.

Questions on each examination paper are chosen from a question bank that is regularly updated. Questions and question papers may be used more than once and therefore providers, candidates or invigilators are not permitted to retain copies of the exam papers.

In order to prepare candidates properly for the examination, all accredited course providers are supplied with a sample examination paper and marking grid. Exams taken computer-based or web-based are automatically marked and the result notified to the candidate immediately. For paper-based exams, the papers are returned to the Examination Institute or Agent to be marked.

In order to pass, candidates must score 26 marks or higher. If a candidate fails, the candidate may retake the exam. There is no limit to the number of times a candidate may retake the examination.

Obviously, the pass rates fluctuate. Since the introduction of the Practitioner examinations for clusters of processes the pass rate of the Practitioner exams has been approximately between 65 and 75 per cent.

Most candidates will take the exam on the completion of the training course. Course providers may cooperate with an Accredited Examination Center (AEC) to provide the examination at their venue. The AEC will be responsible for safeguarding the integrity of the exam process and for returning completed papers to the EI or EA. Examination Institutes and Agents will typically also offer a public schedule of events, when candidates may register and then take the exam.

Any special conditions for holding exams outside the base country of the EI/EA, such as extended lead times, will be published by the examination body.

8.2.3 Dispute
Students with disputes shall pursue these with the appropriate Course Provider, Examination Institute or Examination Agent. Each Examination Institute and Examination Agent has a dispute resolution procedure (DRP) covering its relationship with Course Providers and students. This resolution is made publicly available; e.g. via a website.

8.3 Preparing for the Practitioner Release & Control exam
To enhance your chances for success in the examinations for the ITSM Practitioner Certificate there are several precautions you can take, the first one being to take the examination seriously.

8.3.1 Preparation for the exam
- Join in an accredited training course. Learning the basics of IT Service Management is more fun and more effective if done in a group of professionals sharing experiences and with an experienced tutor with a depth of understanding and practical working experience.
- Plan to spend enough time for private study and revision of course materials, ITIL books and this training guide. As a rule of thumb, you are advised to spend about 30 hours for private study.
- Discuss what you learned in the training course and from the books with colleagues and friends. Sharing experiences about best practice helps you to understand IT Service Management principles.
- Use the most recent sample paper from your exam body to prepare yourself for the type of questions used in the Foundation examination.

8.3.2 Practical assignments
Roughly speaking there are three ways to accomplish the practical assignments:
- as part of a publicly scheduled Practitioner training course;
- as part of the work experience part of a Practitioner training;
- as part of an on-the-job training program.

The assignments in a training course can be part of case study or a virtual environment (e.g. simulation). The main idea behind the introduction of the assignments in such training is to ensure that the attendees will be able to experience the role of a Practitioner, demonstrate their skills and get professional feedback from the course tutor(s).

Some Practitioner courses are offered in close cooperation with the employer(s) of the attendees. In such cases the students working environment may be used for the practical assignments. The advantage of this approach is that real life assignments can be used and feedback and improvement of skills will be directly applicable in practice. The coach assigning the task and providing the feedback could be an experienced colleague or superior of the student, as long as the training provider takes the ultimate responsibility for the quality of the assignments and the feedback.

The third option is the most challenging: learning as an improvement program in action. In such a program a Release & Control team is supported by an experienced coach/trainer to improve the Release & Control processes by learning in practice and from practical experience. The result of the program is a set of improved processes and a group of trained professionals.

Variants and combinations of these options do exist, but the overall message is that the practical assignments are an integral part of the Practitioner training, if not the most valuable part, and, if properly done, will provide a life time learning experience.

8.3.3 Preparation for the day of the exam

- Plan your journey to the examination center. Aim to arrive fifteen minutes early to have a quiet start to the examination, for example with a coffee or tea.
- Have a good nights sleep and start the examination session well rested. Do not try to study the course material until deep into the night.
- Choose clothes that make you feel comfortable, you don't have to represent your company, you are representing yourself.
- Don't forget to bring a valid personal ID paper (passport, ID card).

8.3.4 Hints and tips during the exam

- Carefully read all the questions.
- Start answering the easy questions first.
- In answering the multiple-choice questions, first try to think of an answer yourself before choosing one of the options. Remember, your first hunch is often the best.
- Remember that only one of the provided options is the correct answer. Choose the one which most accurately answers the precise question asked. This answer may not necessarily reflect everything you learned about the subject.
- Don't complicate the question by trying to find counter-examples for the answer you think is best. The questions are not meant to be tricky and in exceptional circumstances, most answers will almost certainly turn out not to be the whole truth.
- Before the end of the examination session, check whether you have answered all the questions. If you are not sure, try your best choice.
- Don't panic. With the right kind of preparation, the examination is not very difficult, you can do it!

8.4 Sample Questions

The following set of sample questions is drawn from the EXIN IT Service Management Practitioner: Release & Control examinations. These questions are a good example of the kind of questions one may expect in the real examinations and can be used to make your study of the Introduction book more effective.

For extra exam preparation one can obtain the most recent sample paper from the examination bodies or an accredited training provider. The most recent sample papers from the Examination Institutes reflect the latest changes and improvements in the examinations or contain an annotated version of the answer key, with comments and explanations for each of the options.

Question 1

You have just started setting up Configuration Management. Together with an external consultant, you have drawn up a Configuration Management plan. This plan has been approved by the Board of Management. In the Configuration Management plan, you have indicated the activities you are going to carry out in the coming period.

Activities
- Analyze existing Configuration Management situation
- Analyze existing configuration data
- Draw up functional specifications for Configuration Management Database (CMDB) and Configuration Management tools
- Select, evaluate and purchase CMDB and Configuration Management tools
- Set up coding system, attributes and naming conventions
- Set up and test CMDB and Configuration Management tools
- Set up space for storage of Configuration Items (CIs) and the Definitive Software Library (DSL)
- Convert all existing data to the new CMDB
- Label all existing CIs
- Carry out initial verification of the CMDB
- Work with new CMDB and Configuration Management tools

Which activity must you definitely add to the above if you want your efforts to be successful?
A. draw up a Release policy document
B. the collection of information using inventory tools
C. the development of procedures and work instructions

Question 2

As a member of the Release and Control team, you are given the task to develop, with specifics, the existing Change Management procedure using work instructions. A work instruction is a guide on how to carry out a procedure.

Objective	*******
Target group	Change Manager
Instruction	After testing the Change for production, the test report must be submitted to the Change Manager. The Change Manager will use the test report, the implementation plan, the existing back-out plan and the necessary documentation to determine whether the Change can be released. The Change Manager will release the Change and register the status in the Change registration system.l

Which step in the "Release Changes" work instruction is missing?
A. informing those involved
B. reviewing the Change
C. planning the back-out

Question 3
Last week two members of the Change Management staff had a discussion with a colleague from Configuration Management staff about responsibility for updating Change logs. They brought up several possibilities.

Which is the proper one?
A   Change involves a transformation in the status of a Configuration Item (CI), so only the Change Manager is responsible for updating its status in the Service Management tool.
B.   A Change involves a transformation in the status of a Configuration Item (CI), so only the Configuration Manager is responsible for updating its status in the Service Management tool.
C.   A Change involves a transformation in the Change process, so only the Change Manager is responsible for updating its status in the Service Management tool.

Question 4
Which of the following Key Performance Indicators (KPIs) does not reflect an improvement in the effectiveness and efficiency of the Release and Control processes?
A.   a percentage improvement in overall duration of the Change Advisory Board (CAB) meeting
B.   a percentage improvement in the speed and accuracy of configuration audits
C.   a reduction in the 'cost' of failed Changes

Question 5
Which of the following metrics is useful in assisting you to determine the effectiveness of the Change Management process?
A.   an increase in the number of recorded Request for Changes (RFCs) per period
B.   an increase in the number of rejected Request for Changes (RFCs)
C.   an increase in the number of Request for Changes (RFCs) being built

Question 6
A system development project was recently started. The Project Manager has asked the Release Manager to demonstrate the effectiveness of this process during the implementation stage.

Which Key Performance Indicator (KPI) will be used in the report?
A. accurate distribution of Releases
B. secure and accurate management of the Definitive Software Library (DSL)
C. the planned composition of Releases matching the actual composition

Question 7

At organization "X" the various business managers usually communicate directly with the developers and programmers when they require new functionalities. You have been tasked to communicate to the business about following the Release and Control processes, and to submit their requests to the Change Management process.

Which of the following best reflects the tone of your communication to the business managers?
A. You have to be firm and enforce the process. Business managers must submit their Change Requests to the change process. There will be severe repercussions for not following the process.
B. You need to create a communication plan outlining the benefits of the Release and Control processes so that resources can be properly planned and Changes documented, assessed and implemented.
C. You need to explain the various categories of Changes to the business managers and allow them to submit standard pre-approved Changes directly to the developers/programmers as most requests for functionalities are minor in nature.

Question 8

Financial Management for IT Services wants to reduce the Total Cost of Ownership for client machines in the organization.

Which information does Financial Management for IT Services need from Configuration Management?
A. Asset Management information regarding the desktop PCs, laptops and software
B. Configuration Management information regarding all hardware
C. Configuration Management information regarding all hardware and software

Question 9

License management is part of the Release and Control processes.

Which process has to verify the software with the accompanying licenses?
A. Change Management
B. Configuration Management
C. Release Management

Question 10

Each Configuration Item (CI) must be given a unique identification code. This code identifies the CI in the Configuration Management Database (CMDB) and is also the code that is physically affixed to the CI by means of a label. You decide to use the following coding for the PCs: WS-UT1-XXX, where UT1 stands for the Utrecht branch, 1st floor, and XXX is a three-digit serial number.

Is this a correct naming convention?

A. No, this code contains too much unnecessary and dynamic information, which can all be found in the CMDB.

B. Yes, by including the branch and floor in the code, in the case of failure it can be seen straight away where the problem is located.

C. Yes, in view of the limited growth of the branches, a three-digit serial number is more than adequate.

Question 11

You want to be able to display the entire life cycle of a Configuration Item (CI), from order to deletion, by giving it a status.

Which is a correct way to do this?

A. ORDERED, STOCK, TEST, LIVE, REPAIR, ARCHIVED, DELETED

B. ORDERED, STOCK, TEST, PRODUCTION, OUT OF ORDER, ARCHIVED, DELETED

C. Request for Change (RFC), STOCK, TEST, LIVE, OUT OF ORDER, ARCHIVED, DELETED

Question 12

What serves as input for the design, build and configuration of a Release?

A. accepted Releases after successful testing

B. Release assembly instructions

C. Release definition and Release plans

Question 13

New software is implemented in a distributed environment. One of the objectives is to ensure the option of fast back-out from Changes across the network.

What needs to be in place to ensure this fast back-out?

A. limited software installation on workstations

B. the possibility to freeze failing applications

C. single user sign-on to all systems

Question 14

The Configuration Management Database (CMDB) is updated and referred to throughout the Release Management process.

Should the definition of planned Releases be recorded in the CMDB?

A. No, because the definition of planned Releases is not a Configuration Item (CI).

B. No, because the definition of planned Releases is not yet an update of the information in the CMDB.

C. Yes, because the definition of planned Releases is the basis for the design, build and configuration of the Release.

Question 15

What does the Definitive Hardware Store (DHS) contain?

A. hardware spare parts for maintaining the systems

B. hardware spares to be used for additional systems or for the recovery of major Incidents

C. information about hardware to roll-out as part of a Release

Question 16

The general IT Manager has noticed that staff are spending a lot of time reviewing Changes.

What is a purpose of Change reviews?

A. to establish that all Changes have been assessed and prioritized

B. to establish that the Change was implemented on time and within the specified cost limitations

C. to establish that the Forward Schedule of Changes (FSC) has been produced and distributed on time

Question 17

What is an activity when reviewing a roll-out plan?

A. check if the roll-out plan requires any adjustment of the organizations release policy

B. check if the roll-out plan fits in with established Service Management and Support procedures

C. check if the roll-out plan has been authorized by the Change requester

Question 18

The Change Management staff is swamped with mail messages from Change builders, testers and other staff reporting the status or progress of specific Changes.

How can this be prevented?

A. ask Change builders, testers and other staff to hold back until the Change is ready for implementation

B. allocate more Change Management staff

C. authorize Change builders, testers and other staff to add information to Change records

Question 19

A car manufacturer has a number of branches worldwide. The management wants to use Voice Over IP to reduce costs. The IT Service Organization is asked to provide this new service.

What are the consequences for the Change, Release and Configuration Management procedures?

A. adjustment of the Change Management plan

B. an extension of the Configuration Management Database (CMDB)

C. none, just another service to manage

Question 20

The Service Manager has issued an audit of the Change Management process for compliance with all Service Support processes next month.

Which item should be included in the examination?
A. Change Advisory Board (CAB) minutes
B. Change model
C. Request for Change (RFC) form

Annex A How Release & Control can work with Application and ICT Infrastructure Management

A.1 What is Application and ICT Infrastructure Management?

There are no agreed definitions for Application or ICT Infrastructure Management, however there are some aspects that most definitions cover in whole or in part, for example:

Application Management

This often refers to the management methods (tools, techniques, processes and resources) that are required to:

- help identify the application requirement;
- help to plan, design and build an application or portfolio of applications;
- help to ensure the applications are deployed, operated, supported and optimized in a properly controlled manner until they are retired from service.

In some environments, Application Management is considered to be a key contributor and major component of IT Strategy Planning, Programme, Design, Transition, Change and Continual Service Improvement Management. In others, the focus is just on the single application development and service management aspects.

Information and Communications Technology Infrastructure Management (ICTIM)

ICTIM covers the processes, organization and tools that are needed to provide a stable IT and Communication infrastructure upon which the applications and related services will run.

Release & Control is vital for Application Management, ICT Infrastructure Management, IT Service Delivery and IT Service Support.

There are 'best practice' methods that help to manage applications and the ICT components throughout much of the life cycle including: ITIL® Application Management; the Application Services Library, ASL; and ITIL® ICT Infrastructure Management. Other methods focus on key areas only, for example CMMI-SW has a strong emphasis on process improvement; RUP concentrates on development and Prince2® on project management aspects only.

A.2 The relevance to Release & Control Practitioners

In many environments Release & Control is activated far too late with consequential additional risks and extra costs to the business.

As Change, Configuration and Release Management are directly affected by new applications as well as by those which are already operational and subject to change, staff involved in Release & Control must have early involvement in the application and ICT planning, development and specification phases. How much involvement will depend on the technologies used, the development approach, the supplier requirements, the organizational culture and the complexity and criticality of the applications and technologies.

The following suggestions are based on experience and good commonsense, they should apply in most situations. We focus on the common generic requirements, design and build phases here.

Release & Control role when identifying and specifying requirements and designing and planning potential solutions

As the Release & Control team owns the CMDB, they must work with the developers to help identify change, configuration, and release requirements for the new application(s) and supporting technologies. As a minimum this means Release & Control will help to:

- identify the ICT infrastructure requirements the application will need to run on;
- specify and agree the types of changes that may be required to be managed 'operationally';
- identify how applications should be released;
- understand the associated dependencies (servers, buildings, networks, contracts, skills etc)

Release & Control role during the Design phase

The Release & Control team works with the application development team and other ICT Infrastructure Management by providing advice on how to move (transition) the application or other technologies from the provider / development / test area into the live production environment.

They need to assure themselves that:

- the design will meet organizational standards for an acceptable configuration;
- designers ensure that 'easy' change and release mechanisms are built into the application; some of this can be provided with the help of application instrumentation and automatic registration.

Early collaboration with designers also helps the Release & Control team to manage the operational and ongoing identification, change control, usage, license tracking, accessibility and status reporting of the application or other ICT 'managed object'.

Release & Control role during the Build phase

During the Build phase Release & Control will focus on collaborating with application development and ICT Infrastructure Management to ensure that the deliverables:

- conform with Configuration Management standards - such as only using tools that are included within the product catalogue;
- are built and tested against the corporate Change and Release Management process;
- have a complete audit trail to show all actions from initiation to deployment.

Once the ICT or application 'managed object' is deployed, then 'normal' Release & Control processes, as described in the earlier chapters within this book, take complete control.

Release & Control plays a significant role in Application and ICT Infrastructure Management, especially in environments where a service life cycle approach is being adopted and integrated management tools (covering Configuration Management and many other areas) are being deployed.

Annex B Process modeling techniques

B.1 ARCI

The ARCI matrix or model, sometimes called RACI or even RASCI, is a simple tool for assigning cross-functional responsibilities. It is a helpful tool during an organizational process design to formalize roles and responsibilities. The objective of the model is to define who does what to make the process work.

ARCI is an abbreviation standing for:
- **A**ccountable - role or person who gets the praise when everything works or who gets the ultimate blame when the work is not satisfactory;
- **R**esponsible - role or person who owns the activity, who does the work;
- (**S**upportive) - role or person who can play a supporting role in implementation;
- **C**onsulted - role or person who should be consulted for information or capability in order to complete the work;
- **I**nformed - role or person who should be informed of the results of the activity.

Typical steps to be followed:
1. Identify and list all the main activities of the process being analyzed. Place those on the left hand side of the matrix.
2. Identify and list all the roles of the process being analyzed. Place those along the top of the matrix.
3. Fill out the matrix.
4. Resolve the conflicts around the Rs:
   - there can only be one Responsible per activity;
   - each activity should have one Responsible.
5. Place the As knowing that:
   - a Responsible can also be Accountable for an activity;
   - the Accountability can be assigned at the process level instead of one doing it for each activity.

The end result should be a matrix that looks like this:

	Role 1	Role 2	Role 3	Role 4	Role 5	Role 6	Role 7
Activity 1	C	A/R	I			I	
Activity 2	C			C		A/R	
Activity 3	C			A		R	
Activity 4	A			R	C	C	
Activity 5	A	C	R	I			
Activity 6	R				I		I

B.2 Flow chart

A flow chart is defined as a graphical representation of the sequence of activities composing a process. It shows what comes first, second, third, etc. It usually describes what the audience will do, if anything, and what happens next. It is a simple yet proven form of process documentation. Four types of flowcharts exist: top-down flowchart, detailed flowchart, workflow diagram and deployment chart.

Being a graphical representation, the following symbols are common in flowchart diagrams (most flowchart tools comes with predefined symbols to select from when building the flowchart).

Start / End

This symbol is used to indicate both the beginning(s) and the end(s) of the process.

Process / Activity

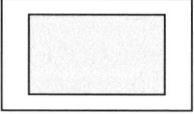

This symbol is used to indicate an activity or a sub-process.

Decision

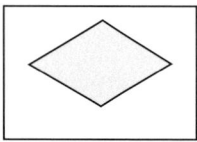

This symbol is used when there is a decision to be taken in the flow. Usually, it is written in the form of a Yes/No question and will result in branching flow lines depending upon the answer.

Reference marker

This symbol is a reference marker. It is usually used to go to a different page or to another line of the flowchart to avoid cross-over with existing links.

B.3 Swim lane

The Swim lane is a technique for mapping roles or organizational structure to processes. It is a popular method, whereby bands or lanes are placed on a page representing steps for a particular role, group or organization.

Here is an example:

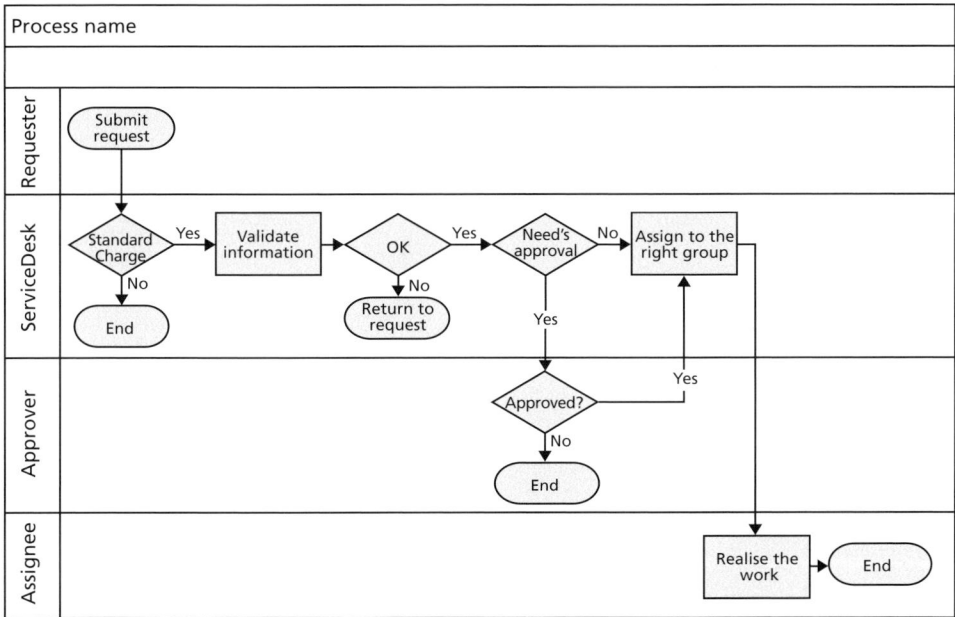

Figure B1   Swim Lane

Annex C Management frameworks

C.1 Quality system: ISO 20000

As the IT Service Management industry cross national boundaries with many organizations dependent on services from many different countries, the ISO/IEC 20000 Information Technology Service Management -1 and -2 offers a method of unifying and defining best practice and high quality services. This standard is the joint effort of the International Organization for Standardization (ISO) and the International Electrotechnical Commission (IEC).

Building on existing national standards (the BS15000-1/-2, 2003 from Britain, which were copied into the AS8018.1/.2, 2004 from Australia and SA15000 in South Africa), this set is the first standard for IT Service Management, and is fully compatible and supportive of the ITIL framework. It covers the majority of the total expenditure that IT Groups spend to provide products and services.

Scope of ISO/IEC 20000-1 and -2

This standard 'promotes the adoption of an integrated process approach to effectively deliver managed services to meet the business and customer requirements'. An - integrated process approach – means that an organization needs to identify and manage all of its numerous activities, group them into business processes and interlink such processes together.

The ISO/IEC is composed of two parts.
ISO/IEC 20000 part 1: *Specification* for Service Management has 10 sections and 19 Objectives (represented in second-level bullets) which are:
- **Scope**
- **Terms and definitions**
- **Requirements for a management system**
  - 'To provide a management system, including policies and a framework to enable the effective management and implementation of all IT services.'
- **Planning and implementing Service Management**
  - 'To plan the implementation and delivery of Service Management.'
  - 'To implement the Service Management objectives and plan.'
  - 'To monitor, measure and review that the Service Management objectives and plan are being achieved.'
  - 'To improve the effectiveness and efficiency of Service Delivery and Management.'
- **Planning and implementing new or changed services**
  - 'To ensure that the new services and changes to services will be deliverable and manageable at the right cost and service delivery.'
- **Service delivery process**
  - 'To define, agree, record and manage levels of services.'
  - 'To produce agreed timely, accurate reports for informed decision making and effective communication.'
  - 'To insure that agreed service continuity and availability to customers can be met in all circumstances.'

- – 'To budget and account for the cost of service provision.'
- – 'To ensure that the service provider has, at all times, sufficient capacity to meet the current and future agreed demands of the customer's needs.'
- – 'To manage information security effectively within all service activities' [with reference to ISO/IEC 17799].
- **Relationship processes**
  - – 'To establish and maintain a good relationship between the service provider and the customer based on understanding the customer and their business drivers.'
  - – 'To manage suppliers to ensure the provision of seamless, quality services.'
- **Resolution processes**
  - – 'To restore agreed service to the business as soon as possible or to respond to service requests.'
  - – 'To minimize disruption to the business by proactive identification and by analysis of the cause of service incidents, and by managing problems to closure.'
- **Control processes**
  - – 'To define and control the components of the service and infrastructure and maintain accurate configuration information.'
  - – 'To ensure all changes are assessed, approved, implemented and reviewed in a controlled manner.'
- **Release process**
  - – 'To deliver, distribute and track one or more changes in a release into the live environment.'

Further to providing for standardized terminology and processes to be used by all, 20000-2 provides guidance to auditors and offers assistance to organizations planning service improvements or to be audited.

ISO/IEC 20000 part 2: Code of practice for Service Management has also 10 sections and 19 Objectives (represented in second-level bullets) which are:
- **Scope**
- **Terms and definitions**
- **The management system**
  - – 'To provide a management system, including policies and a framework to enable the effective management and implementation of all IT services.'
  - – 'To ensure that Service Management personnel are competent to undertake their role.'
- **Planning and implementing Service Management**
  - – 'To plan the implementation and delivery of Service Management.'
  - – 'To implement the Service Management objectives and plan.'
  - – 'To monitor, measure and review that the Service Management objectives and plan are being achieved.'
  - – 'To improve the effectiveness and efficiency of Service Delivery and Management.'
  - – 'To ensure that the new services and changes to services will be deliverable and manageable at the agreed cost and service quality.'
- **Planning and implementing new or changed services**
- **Service Delivery processes**
  - – 'To define, agree, record and manage levels of services.'

- 'To produce agreed timely, reliable, accurate reports for informed decision-making and effective communication.'
- 'To insure that agreed service and availability to customers can be met in all circumstances.'
- 'To budget and account for the cost of service provision.'
- 'To ensure that the service provider has, at all times, sufficient capacity to meet the current and future agreed demands of customer's business needs.'
- 'To manage information security effectively within all service activities'[reference to ISO/IEC 17799].
- **Relationship processes**
  - 'To establish and maintain a good relationship between the service provider and customer, based on understanding the customer and their business drivers.'
  - 'To manage supplier(s) to ensure the provision of seamless, quality services.'
- **Resolution processes**
  - 'To restore normal service as soon as possible or to respond to service requests.'
  - 'To minimize disruption to the business by proactive identification of the cause of service incidents and by managing problems to closure.'
- **Control processes**
  - 'To define and control the components of the service and infrastructure and maintain accurate configuration information.'
  - 'To ensure all changes are assessed, approved, implemented and reviewed in a controlled manner.'
- **Release process**
  - 'To deliver, distribute and track one or more changes in a release into the live environment.'

ISO/IEC 20000 for the control processes[5]

Change and Configuration Management are two core processes in the process model. These processes enable a service provider to control the components of the service and infrastructure, and maintain accurate information on the configuration. This accurate information is a basic requirement for decision making in the Change Management process, as well as for all other processes in the IT service organization.

Configuration Management

Objective: To define and control the components of the service and infrastructure, and maintain accurate configuration information.[6]

Note: Financial asset accounting falls outside of the scope of Configuration Management.

There shall be an integrated approach to Change and Configuration Management planning. Configuration Management shall provide information to the Change Management process on the impact of a requested change on the service and infrastructure configurations.

---

5 From: ISO/IEC 20000, a pocket guide, pg 57-62, Van Haren Publishing, 2006
6 The text in Italics refers to the prescriptive txt originating from part I of ISO 20000 (Specification) and the other text refers to part II (Code of practice)

What are defined as a configuration item and its components are documented in a policy. Methods for identifying, controlling and tracking of components is provided by Configuration Management.

All configuration items shall be uniquely identified and defined to describe their functional and physical characteristics. The information to be recorded for each item shall be defined and shall include the relationships and documentation necessary for effective Service Management. The configuration management database (CMDB) shall be actively managed and verified to ensure its reliability and accuracy.

Changes to configuration items e.g. changes and movements of software and hardware shall be traceable and auditable.

To protect its integrity the CMDB shall be held in a secure environment which prevents unauthorized access, provides means for disaster recovery and permits the retrieval of copies of the controlled masters, e.g. software and support documents. Configuration control procedures shall ensure that the integrity of systems, services and service components is maintained.

Configuration audit procedures shall include:
* *recording deficiencies;*
* *methods on improvement actions;*
* *reporting on the outcome.*

All major assets and configurations should have a responsible manager who ensures appropriate protection and control, e.g. changes are authorized before implementation.

A configuration plan should include:
* scope, objectives, policy, roles and responsibilities;
* definition, recording and reporting of configuration items;
* requirements for accountability, traceability, auditability, e.g. for security or legal or business purposes;
* configuration control, e.g. owner of the configuration item, access, protection, version and release control.

Items that should be registered in the configuration management database (CMDB) include:
* issues and releases of systems and software and related documentation, e.g. requirements specifications, test reports, release documentation and ownership;
* configuration baselines or build statements for applicable environment, standard hardware builds and release;
* master hardcopy and electronic libraries;
* licenses and security components e.g firewalls, secure magnetic media;
* service related documentation, e.g. SLAs;
* service supporting facilities, e.g. power to computer room;
* relationships and dependencies between configuration items.

Configuration information should be kept current and made available for planning, decision making and managing changes to the defined configuration. Configuration Management reports should be made available to all relevant parties. Reports should cover latest configuration item versions, location of item, interdependencies and version history.

Verification and audit processes should be scheduled to ensure that the service provider:
• is in control of its configurations, master copies and licenses;
• protects its physical and intellectual capital;
• provides confidence that configuration information is accurate, controlled and visible;
• provides changes, releases and environments which conform to specified requirements.

Configuration audits should be held to check on performance and functional characteristics of specified configuration documents (functional audit) as well as to verify that configuration items conform to their product 'as built/produced' specifications (physical audit). Deficiencies and non-conformities should be recorded and fed back to the relevant parties.

> **Example assessment questions:**
> • *Is there a well understood policy defining what constitutes a configuration item?*
> • *Do procedures prevent configuration records being added, modified, replaced or removed without appropriate authority or controlling documentation?*
> • *Are regular and accurate reports produced for management?*

Change Management
Objective: To ensure all changes are assessed, approved, implemented and reviewed in a controlled manner.

Changes, like new releases, version updates, hardware moves, or changes resulting from incident/problem solutions, do have their impact on the IT service environment.
To ensure that all changes are approved, implemented and reviewed in a controlled manner, Change Management controls the processing of all changes to the infrastructure.

All changes shall be recorded and classified (e.g. urgent, major, minor) and the process shall provide procedures, which include:
• *a defined and documented scope for all service and infrastructural changes;*
• *assessment of changes for risks, impact and business benefits;*
• *the manner in which unsuccessful changes shall be reversed or remedied;*
• *policies and procedures for emergency changes;*
• *change scheduling, monitoring and reporting;*
• *approval, checking, scheduling and controlling of the implementation of changes;*
• *a post implementation review.*

Change records shall be analyzed regularly to detect increasing levels of changes, frequently recurring change categories, emerging trends and other relevant information.
All changes shall be reviewed for success or failure after implementation. Results of reviews shall be fed into the service improvement plan.

A schedule that contains details of all the changes approved for implementation and their proposed implementation dates shall be maintained and communicated to relevant parties.

Scheduling information should be available to the people affected by the change.

A post-implementation review should be undertaken for major changes to check that:
1. the change met its objectives;
2. the customers are contented with the results;
3. there have been no unexpected side effects.

Deficiencies identified in a review of the Change Management process should be fed into the plans for improving the service.

> **Example assessment questions:**
> • *Are there formal procedures to ensure that all changes are approved, checked and implemented in a controlled manner?*
> • *Are change records analyzed regularly to detect increasing levels of change, frequently recurring types, emerging trends and other relevant information?*

ISP/IEC 20000 for the release process[7]

While Change Management is focused at controlling changes, Release Management delivers the planned changes. Release Management should be integrated with the Configuration and Change Management processes to ensure tuning and settling of releases and executed changes. Release Management coordinates the activities of the service provider, suppliers and the business to plan and deliver a release in the IT environment.

Release Management Process

Objective: To deliver, distribute and track one or more changes in a release into the live environment.

Note: The Release Management process should be integrated with the Configuration and Change Management processes.

Good planning and management are essential to successfully distribute a release and to manage the associated impact and risks.

The Release Policy stating frequency and type of releases shall be documented and agreed.

The Release Policy should define:
• the roles and responsibilities;
• the authority for releasing versions into acceptance, test and production environments;
• the unique identification, description, verification and acceptance of all releases;
• the approach to grouping changes into a release;

---

7   ISO/IEC 20000, a pocket guide, pg 62-68, Van Haren Publishing, 2006

- the approach to automating the build, installation and release distribution processes to aid repeatability and efficiency.

The service provider shall plan the release of services, systems, software and hardware. Plans how to roll-out the release shall be agreed and authorized by all relevant parties e.g. customers, users operations and support staff. The roll-out plan shall include:
- *recording of release date and deliverables;*
- *references to related change requests, known errors and problems;*
- *the manner in which the release is remedied if unsuccessful;*
- *communication to Incident Management.*

The roll-out plan may also define:
- identification of dependencies;
- communication, preparation, documentation and training for customer and support staff;
- verification and acceptance;
- release and sign off;
- scheduling of post-release audits.

All documentation on new releases is according to the requirements of the CMDB. After successful installation the Asset and Configuration Management records shall be updated. Change Management shall execute a post-implementation review. Recommendations shall be fed into the service improvement plan.

Release and distribution shall be designed and implemented so that the integrity of hardware and software is maintained during installation, handling, packaging and delivery. A controlled acceptance test environment shall be established to build and test all releases prior to distribution.

Information systems and software releases from in-house teams, system builders or other organizations are verified on receipt.
The release and distribution are designed to:
- conform with the systems architecture, Service Management and infrastructural standards;
- identify risks, so remedial actions can be taken if required;
- enable verification that the target platform satisfies prerequisites before installation;
- enable verification that a release is complete when it reaches its destination.

The output from this process is used for testing and includes release notes, installation instructions, installed software and hardware with related configuration baseline.
The end result is signed-off on completeness against requirements.

Verification and acceptance processes should:
- verify that the controlled acceptance test environment matches the requirements of target production environments;
- ensure that the release is created from versions under Configuration Management;
- verify that the testing has been completed, e.g. functional and non-functional tests, business acceptance test, testing of build, release, distribution and installation procedures;

- ensure that the release is tested to the satisfaction of customers and service provider staff;
- ensure that the release authority signs off each stage of acceptance testing;
- Verify that the target platform satisfies the hardware and software prerequisites and that a release is complete when it reaches its destination.

> **Example assessment questions:**
> • *Are there appropriate and comprehensive plans on how to roll-out a release to each site and user, agreed and signed off by all potentially affected parties?*
> • *Are all releases built and tested in a controlled acceptance test environment before release?*

C.2 Process maturity: CMMI

The Capability Maturity model (CMM) was published by the Software Engineering Institute (of Carnegie Mellon University) and was originally applied to the ability of an organization to improve the maturity of the software creation processes. One of its basic premises is the notion that the entity will evolve to different maturity levels by establishing different processes in an evolutive manner to consistently improve results.

A similar Maturity Model has been established by the European Foundation for Quality Management (EFQM), established in 1988 by several major European companies, with the endorsement of the European Commission. The EFQM also defines a standard model for those wishing to achieve IT service excellence supported by a program of continual improvement.

The Software Engineering Institute (SEI) model rates process maturity on an organizational basis. It sets baselines that define the state of maturity of a given organization with respect to its application of processes to manage Service Delivery and Service Support as defined within ITIL. It can be used to assess a whole organization, a business unit, a line of business or a large project.

The model is characterized by the following states of Maturity which were developed based on the typical evolution of organizations on their road to continual quality improvement:

- **Level 1 – Initial** - The overall process is ad-hoc and occasionally even chaotic. Few processes are defined and success depends on individual effort.
- **Level 2 – Repeatable** - Basic processes are established to track performance and proper disciplines are in place to repeat earlier successes.
- **Level 3 - Defined** - Process definitions are established and standardized throughout the organization, the processes interfaces are defined in a way that the various processes and resources work well integrated with each other. Different projects or circumstances are able to tailor the standard processes to their specific requirements.
- **Level 4 - Quantitatively Managed** - Detailed measures for the software processes and their results are monitored and acted-on through a well established measurement and performance management program.
- **Level 5 – Optimizing** - Continual process improvement is enabled by quantitative feedback from the process. The continual improvement program is well established with defined activities, responsibilities, improvement objectives and reviews, and it is aligned to the overall business goals and objectives.

One key feature of the SEI CMM model is that it provides only one rating for the entire organization or business unit. This model will not segregate the sub component units or departments on the assumption that the maturity of the organization is only as strong as the weakest link.

This adaptation of the SEI Maturity Model, restricted to the ITIL core processes, needs to consider the road to maturity in achieving service quality for the organizations. Typically, the implementation and integration of some of the ITSM processes is gradual, resulting in progressive process scope at different Maturity Levels.

A common presentation of this model is based on a 'Radar' or 'Spiderweb' diagram, with the ITSM processes represented as radiating from a central hub. The maturity of each process is represented by the distance from the central hub. This measurement is often made by utilizing a checklist of questions designed to measure the key attributes of each CMMI level. The following diagram illustrates the distribution of ITSM processes in the Capability Maturity Model:

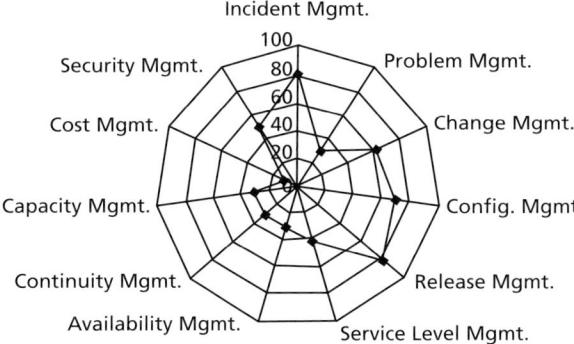

Figure C1   ITSM process Performance

C.3 Audit framework: CobiT®

The IT Governance Institute (ITGI) has developed CobiT® as a framework to provide guidance to IT auditors and business management with regard to the control of IT resources. The stated mission of the ITGI is:

'To research, develop, publicize and promote an authoritative, up-to-date, international set of generally accepted IT Control Objectives for day-to-day use by business managers and auditors.'

The goal of the CobiT framework is to define standard Control Objectives for Information and related Technology that meet the multiple needs of management by bridging the gaps between business risks, control needs and technical issues. CobiT defines requirements for good practices across a domain and process framework and presents activities in a manageable and logical structure. The definition of 'good practices' is: 'consensus of experts that will help optimize information investments and will provide a measure to be judged against when things do go wrong.'

Management is charged with the responsibility to establish an internal control system or framework that supports the business processes, making it clear how each individual control activity satisfies the information requirements and impacts the IT resources. Impact on IT resources is highlighted in the CobiT Framework together with the business requirements for effectiveness, efficiency, confidentiality, integrity, availability, compliance and reliability of information that need to be satisfied. In addition, management has the responsibility to establish, maintain, and monitor Control. 'Control' is defined as 'the creation and maintenance of policies, organizational structures, practices and procedures' that ensure that management directives are complied with. Senior IT management must ensure that necessary governance structures are in place, to ensure that due diligence is exercized by all individuals involved in the management, use, design, development, maintenance or operation of information systems. Within the CobiT Framework, an IT control objective is a statement of the desired result or purpose to be achieved by implementing control procedures within a particular IT activity.

The CobiT Framework consists of a set of 34 high-level Control Objectives, one for each of the IT processes, grouped into four domains:
• Planning and Organization
• Acquisition and Implementation
• Delivery and Support
• Monitoring

The 34 Control Objectives are supported by 318 recommended detailed control objectives. The framework is pictorially represented as follows:

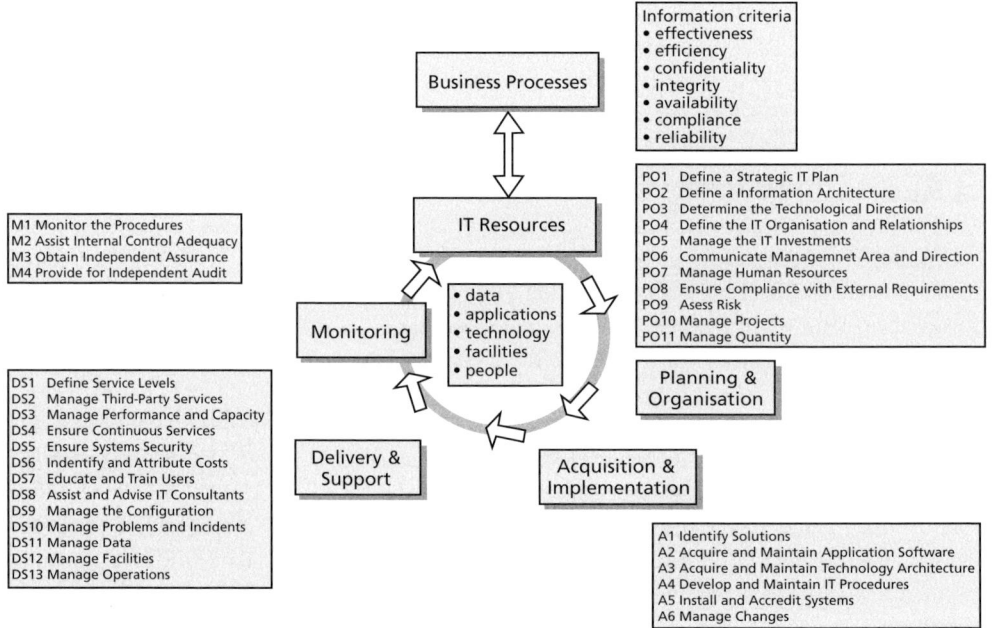

Figure C2   CobiT

CobiT vs ITIL

CobiT was developed from the Audit and Control responsibilities of Management and applies common financial and internal control concepts to the operations of an IT department within a larger entity. CobiT is a recognized standard approach that defines the key activities to be undertaken to achieve control. It is a rigorous and defined approach.

ITIL, by comparison, is a best practice. ITIL (the IT Infrastructure Library) is recognized globally as the most widely accepted approach to IT Service Management in the world, providing a comprehensive and consistent set of best practices for IT Service Management, promoting a quality approach to achieving business effectiveness and efficiency in the use of information systems. As a best practice, there is no mandated requirement to adopt all of the ITSM processes. ITIL is more flexible and adaptable to the requirements of the organization that engages in implementation.

ITIL best practices are well suited to actively implement and manage many of the Control Objectives defined by CobiT. Recent developments in the IT industry have seen the CobiT Control Objectives mapped to the attributes of the ITSM best practices. Through this approach, the requirements of management to achieve control of IT are achieved with the ITIL Service Support and Service Delivery processes.

C.4 MOF

Microsoft Operations Framework (MOF) is the Microsoft approach to IT Service Management. MOF is the framework that describes Microsoft's vision for managing production systems within MS Windows client/server IT environments. MOF is an extension of, with Microsoft specific content, the generally accepted industry best practices spelled out in ITIL. Microsoft built MOF on the 'best practice' language and guidance of ITIL, modified for the 'Microsoft Centric' enterprise. MOF provides best practices for Microsoft technologies; it is scaleable to enable IT specialists to use it across the entire enterprise, and across the modern open IT environment that defines much of the current IT world.

MOF does contain specific recommendations for Microsoft products and technologies, but it can also be applied across the entire enterprise for managing IT Service Delivery and infrastructure. MOF is best described a bridge between generally accepted standard IT Service Management best practice (as defined by ITIL) - and the management of Microsoft applications.

Introduction

MOF is the Microsoft approach IT Service Management guidance and its development aims to address the process, organization, and technical operations demands faced by organizations delivering mission critical services. It also aims to extend the reach and accessibility of operations knowledge available for Microsoft products, through delivery of best practice guidance and white papers.

MOF documents the experience of large IT Operations organizations and solution providers, and documents how they operate service solutions effectively (i.e. developed applications and deployed infrastructure). It has been developed with the help of customers, partners and

Microsoft's own product groups, internal IT operations, consultants and engineers. The global user community has shaped MOFs development.

The MOF framework is defined by three core models - Process, Team and Risk. Each model represents a major component of the day-to-day delivery of IT operations. The management approach to each incorporates principles and practices that business and IT practitioners need to manage IT services and Infrastructure effectively. Together they detail the processes and organizational roles required to minimize risk and achieve high systems reliability, availability, supportability and manageability of service solutions.

Microsoft utilizes the best practices for IT Service Management as defined by ITIL. Microsoft has placed ITIL at the core in the development of MOF, but made the following enhancements:
- MOF is based on ITIL, but also adapts ITIL with specific guidelines for using Microsoft's products and technologies.
- MOF also adapts the ITIL code of practice to support distributed IT environments and emerging IT solutions such as application hosting, mobile-device computing, web-based transaction and e-commerce systems.
- MOF is intended for business people and IT practitioners who run their businesses on a Microsoft platform, who need to interoperate with other technology platforms, and who depend on systems that run across organizational boundaries.
- Consequently, it includes specific guidelines for running on the Microsoft platform in a variety of business scenarios.

MOF constitutes of three interrelated pillars:
1. The MOF Process Model; the processes required to deliver end-to-end services to the customers of the IT department.
2. The MOF Team Model; the coupling between roles within processes and competences required to perform the activities.
3. The MOF Risk Model; the underlying notion of Risk Management in every process, activity and role.

Essentially, MOF extends ITIL with the following components:
- An IT Service Life cycle - this is based on Deming's Plan-Do-Check-Act cycle for quality improvement.
- Time and Event based Reviews - these enable the correct and timely handover of inputs and outputs between the life cycle phases.
- Three core models - Process, Team and Risk.
- Additional and deeper processes.
- Prescriptive guidance.

MOF Quadrants in the MOF Process Model
This life cycle allows the model to be easily integrated with solution development frameworks and methodologies such as Microsoft's Solutions Framework (MSF). This encourages developers to design operability into each service solution they develop and to consider ongoing operational from the outset.

Since these methodologies focus on the development life cycle of a service solution they can be tied to the MOF event based Release Approved and Release Readiness management checkpoints. These checkpoints are covered later in the section on Operation Management Reviews (OMRs).

Although the model suggests a sequential view of activities, through the Changing – Operating – Supporting - Optimizing quadrants, in reality there would normally be a number of service solutions being operated and supported in the production environment. However, at any time there would be a smaller number going through a process of improvement (Optimizing), development and release (Changing).

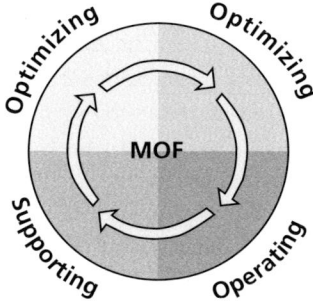

Figure C3   MOF Quadrants

The Quadrants

The four MOF quadrants highlight the processes that teams who are responsible for IT operations must perform to effectively manage IT services and Infrastructure. As part of the design, MOF organizes these processes into logical groupings, known as quadrants of related functions.

The Process Model quadrants each have a specific mission that contributes to the various stages of the IT life cycle. Each also has an explicit Operations Management Review that evaluates the performance of the day-to-day activity of that quadrant or the readiness of that certain quadrant. This means that there are two kinds of OMRs: release based and event based reviews. The Mission of service aims of the Service Management functions, and the Operations Management Review for each quadrant are illustrated below.

Quadrant - Mission of service	Operations Management Review - Aim of SMFs
Changing - The controlled implementation of new service solutions and the controlled adjustment of existing service solutions.	Release Readiness Review-to identify, review, approve, record and incorporate change into a managed IT environment.
Operating - The guarantee of the effectiveness of implemented service solutions.	Operations Review - to monitor, control, manage, and administer service solutions and meet agreed service levels on a daily basis.
Supporting -The Quality Assurance of agreed service levels.	Service Level Agreement (SLA) - to identify, assign, diagnose, track, and resolve incidents, problems, and requests based on agreed service levels.
Optimizing - The Quality Improvement of existing service solutions.	Release Approved Review - to identify possible quality improvements to existing services and to request these to be implemented.

Service Management Functions (SMFs)

Service Management Functions (SMFs) are the underlying processes and activities within each MOF quadrant that support the mission of service for that quadrant. They operate across all service solutions in operation and across the underlying IT infrastructure.

Underlying processes and activities

MOF draws directly from ITIL for many of the SMFs, as it is generally accepted best practice within the industry. ITIL was created to be strategically adopted and tactically adapted within organizations.

MOF adapts all of the ITIL core processes and augments them with additional guidance based on operational experience of Microsoft, its partners and customers. In addition, other key processes have also been included, particularly within the operating quadrant.

MOF also adds one more SMF to the optimizing quadrant, workforce management, that recommends best practice to recruit, retain, reward and motivate the IT operations workforce. By emphasizing its status as a Service Management Function within MOF, Microsoft has highlighted the importance of workforce management beyond the position this received in ITIL.

In MOF a total of 20 essential SMFs are identified, and the Process Model organizes these into four major quadrants, each one representing the highest level of work in the Process Model. Although each SMF's primary mission supports one home quadrant, based on its relevance to the mission of service for that quadrant, SMFs remains cross-quadrant in nature.

Processes, procedures and tasks

In simple terms, Service Management Functions are processes, which are made up of procedures, which in turn are made up of sets of tasks. Sometimes an SMF is composed of a number of sub-processes or second level processes. E.g. the SMF Configuration Management contains the sub-processes Configuration Management planning, Configuration identification, Configuration control, Configuration verification and audit, and Configuration status accounting. These are not sequential steps in one linear process but parallel sets of activities, each leading to its own goal.

In other cases an SMF can be one linear process; e.g. in the case of the SMF Change Management we can find a simple series of sequential steps: Change request, Change classification, Change authorization, Change development, Change release and Change review.

Annex D Correction key multiple choice questions

D.1 Correction Key chapter 5 Configuration Management

Question 1

Which of the following elements does not belong in the CMDB?

The correct answer is C

A. *The technical information about the network switches.*
These are attributes of CIs and belong in the CMDB

B. *The default profiles (access rights) of the systems users*
These default profile are a part of an IT service and defined in a document contained in the CMDB

C. *The program code of an ERP module*
This will belong in the DSL rather than the CMDB

D. *The associations between a software and the PCs on which it is installed*
Relationships between different CIs of the infrastructure are contained in the structure of the CMDB

Question 2

The initial planning Configuration Management includes activities such as

- Gaining agreement on the purpose, objectives, scope, priority and approach for Configuration Management
- Analyzing existing Configuration Management systems, data and processes
- Developing high level Configuration Plan
- Planning for and obtaining financing for a Configuration Management tool and extra resources
- Agreeing on the corporate policy, processes and defining what can be tailored during roll-out

What other activity is part of that phase?

The correct answer is B

A. *Do an initial discovery of all CI*
This only happens after the initial planning was completed

B. *Assign a person to be responsible for Configuration Management*
See section 7.5.1 of Service Support (OGC)

C. *Do the project plan*
This is not part of project management rather than the initial planning

D. *Determine which indicators will be used for process control*
This is part of the implementation of the process rather than the planning of it

Question 3

Different types of relationships with a CI can be found in the CMDB. Which of the following is not an example of relationship that can be found in the CMDB?

The correct answer is C

A. *Relationship between an application and the server it is hosted on*
This relationship is associated with two CIs and therefore should be included in the CMDB

B. *Relationship between a PC and an incident record for that PC*
This relationship is associated with a CI and therefore should be included in the CMDB

C. *Relationship between the incident record for a PC and the solution which was used to correct the incident*
Neither an incident record nor a problem record is considered part of the CMDB. Relating incidents to solutions is not considered part of the CMDB.

D. *Relationship between a server and an RFC to upgrade its operating system*
This relationship is associated with a CI and therefore should be included in the CMDB

Question 4

During the CI control portion of the process, which of the following activities should be taking place?

1. Record new CIs created by the development teams
2. Update existing CIs (attributes, relationships, status etc.) following changes to them
3. Remove from the CMDB, CIs which were removed from the infrastructure
4. Back-up and Archive CMDB data
5. Produce reports on the number of CI in the CMDB and modifications to them
6. Execute periodic verification between the CMDB content and the actual elements in the infrastructure
7. Protecting integrity of configurations
8. Update the CMDB after verifying the existence of physical items

The correct answer is B.

A. 1,2,3,4,5,6
4 is part of the process maintenance rather than the process itself
5 is part of status accounting portion of the process
6 is part of the verification and audit
7 and 8 are missing

B. 1,2,3,7,8
See section 7.6.3 of Service Support (OGC)

C. 6,8
6 is part of the verification and audit
1,2,3,7 are missing

D. 1,2,3,5,7
5 is part of status accounting portion of the process
8 is missing

D.2 Correction Key chapter 6 Release Management

Question 1
Which of the following items will not be found in the DSL?
A. Functional Design of a business application
B. Spare parts
C. A baseline laptop image
D. Program Source Code
The correct answer is B. Spare parts; these may be kept in the DHS.

Question 2
What is the role of the Definitive Software Library (DSL) in the Release Management process?
A. (Physical) Storage of the original versions of all software used
B. Reference work containing all software documentation manuals, etc.
C. Registration tool for all software items
D. Sort of Configuration Management Database (CMDB) for software
The correct answer is A. (Physical) Storage of the original versions of all software used

Question 3
Which activity is part of the Release Management process?
A. Approving a change in Application X from version 1 to version 1.1
B. Put together the release containing the new version 1.1 of Application X
C. To record which computers the new version 1.1 of Application X is installed on
The correct answer is B. Put together the release containing the new version 1.1 of Application X.

Question 4
At which moment does Release Management start building, testing and implementing a change?
A. As soon as the members of the Change Advisory Board (CAB) have discussed the impact analysis
B. As soon as the Request for Change (RFC) has been formally authorized and the planning has been set
C. As soon as the Service Quality Plan has been updated to warrant the quality after the execution of the change
D. As soon as Problem Management files the RFC
The correct answer is B. As soon as the Request for Change (RFC) has been formally authorized and the planning has been set.

D.3 Correction Key chapter 7 Change Management

Question 1
According to the scope of the proposed change, Requests for Change will be processed following predefined change models, e.g. for standard, minor, substantial and major changes. How are these change models to be prepared and authorized?
A. Change models are defined by Change Management and authorized by the CAB

B. Change models are defined by support staff and authorized by the Change Manager
C. Change models are defined by Change Management and authorized by the organization

A.   Incorrect. The change models are in fact procedures and need to be agreed and authorized by the organization.
B.   Incorrect. The support staff may provide the input, especially if specific change models will be used for PCs, network etc. Change models are in fact Change Management procedures and Change Management is responsible for their definition.
C.   Correct. *See Service Support book 8.3.*

Question 2
The project manager responsible for implementing the XYZ application has ordered the roll out of the client software. His project plan has been approved by the CAB at the start of the project. Can the roll out be part of the next release without a Request for Change?
A. No. The project manager lacks the authority to request the implementation and a Request for Change is needed from the organization's management to ensure the implementation is properly authorized.
B. No. The roll out of the client software is a change and needs to be coordinated via Change Management. All Change Management procedures apply, including the need for a Request for Change.
C. Yes. The project manager is responsible for the implementation. The project manager only needs to inform Change Management of the planning of upcoming changes.
D. Yes. The project plan was in fact a Request for Change and the CAB has already agreed.

A.   Incorrect. The project manager will be authorized to raise a Request for Change. In cases like this the authorization of the change is less a problem than the impact analysis, the coordination and the planning.
B.   Correct. *It will usually be impossible to analyze all the risks of the change at the start of the project. To ensure conscious decision taking and minimize risks, also projects should adhere to the Change Management procedures and raise RFCs for changes in the IT Infrastructure.*
C.   Incorrect. This would imply that it would be impossible for Change Management to minimize the risks for all IT services provided.
D.   Incorrect. This may be the practice in some organizations, but it is certainly not advisable. See the comments on the correct answer.

Question 3
What is the difference between the Forward Schedule of Changes (FSC) and the Projected Service Availability (PSA)?
A. The FSC is based on the PSA and not the other way around.
B. The FSC holds information on availability of CIs, the PSA not.
C. The PSA is based on the FSC and not the other way around.
D. The PSA needs to be agreed with the customer, the FSC not.

A . Incorrect. The Projected Service Availability contains details of changes to agreed SLAs and service availability because of the currently planned FSC.
B.   Incorrect. FSC may refer to services but also to detailed infrastructure CI availability, the PSA always relates to services - and services are CIs.

C. Correct. *The FSC contains details of all changes approved for implementation and their proposed implementation dates. The PSA is derived from the FSC.*

D. *Incorrect. Both FSC and PSA need to be agreed with the customer.*
    Practical Assignments

D.4 Correction Key chapter 8 Certification in Release & Control

Question 1

You have just started setting up Configuration Management. Together with an external consultant, you have drawn up a Configuration Management plan. This plan has been approved by the Board of Management.

In the Configuration Management plan, you have indicated the activities you are going to carry out in the coming period.

Activities
- Analyze existing Configuration Management situation
- Analyze existing configuration data
- Draw up functional specifications for Configuration Management Database (CMDB) and Configuration Management tools
- Select, evaluate and purchase CMDB and Configuration Management tools
- Set up coding system, attributes and naming conventions
- Set up and test CMDB and Configuration Management tools
- Set up space for storage of Configuration Items (CIs) and the Definitive Software Library (DSL)
- Convert all existing data to the new CMDB
- Label all existing CIs
- Carry out initial verification of the CMDB
- Work with new CMDB and Configuration Management tools

Which activity must you definitely add to the above if you want your efforts to be successful?
A. draw up a Release policy ocument
B. the collection of information using inventory tools
C. the development of procedures and work instructions

A. *Incorrect. This is a task of Release Management.*
B. *Incorrect. The choice has been made to convert and verify existing data. The use of inventory tools is therefore not strictly necessary. Ref. section 7.5.1 of Service Support (OGC)*
C. Correct. *If it is not clear what the work method is, for the registration of new CIs, changes to existing CIs, etc. because there are no procedures for this and no one has had any training, the CMDB will be inaccurate within a very short time.*

Question 2

As a member of the Release and Control team, you are given the task to develop, with specifics, the existing Change Management procedure using work instructions. A work instruction is a guide on how to carry out a procedure.

Work Instruction "Release Changes"

Objective	*******
Target group	Change Manager
Instruction	After testing the Change for production, the test report must be submitted to the Change Manager. The Change Manager will use the test report, the implementation plan, the existing back-out plan and the necessary documentation to determine whether the Change can be released. The Change Manager will release the Change and register the status in the Change registration system.l

Which step in the "Release Changes" work instruction is missing?
A. informing those involved
B. reviewing the Change
C. planning the back-out

A. **Correct.** *This is done via the Forward Schedule of Changes (FSC). Ref. 8.5 of Service Support (OGC)*
B. *Incorrect. The Change is reviewed after its release.*
C. *Incorrect. A back-out plan is already in the work instruction.*

Question 3

Last week two members of the Change Management staff had a discussion with a colleague from Configuration Management staff about responsibility for updating Change logs. They brought up several possibilities.

Which is the proper one?
A. A Change involves a transformation in the status of a Configuration Item (CI), so only the Change Manager is responsible for updating its status in the Service Management tool.
B. A Change involves a transformation in the status of a Configuration Item (CI), so only the Configuration Manager is responsible for updating its status in the Service Management tool.
C. A Change involves a transformation in the Change process, so only the Change Manager is responsible for updating its status in the Service Management tool.

A. *Incorrect. The Change Manager doesn't update the Configuration Management Database (CMDB), this is the responsibility of Configuration Management.*
B. **Correct.** *A Change involves the transformation in the status of a Configuration Item (CI), registered in the Configuration Management Database (CMDB), and Configuration Management is responsible for updating the CMDB.*
Ref. 8.3 of Service Support (OGC)

C. *Incorrect. A Change involves a transformation in the status of a Configuration Item (CI), not the Change process.*

Question 4
Which of the following Key Performance Indicators (KPIs) does not reflect an improvement in the effectiveness and efficiency of the Release and Control processes?
A. a percentage improvement in overall duration of the Change Advisory Board (CAB) meeting
B. a percentage improvement in the speed and accuracy of configuration audits
C. a reduction in the 'cost' of failed Changes

A. **Correct.** *A reduction in the duration of the CAB meeting has nothing to do with its effectiveness and efficiency in regard to ensuring its quality.*
B. *Incorrect. This can be used as a KPI.*
C. *Incorrect. This can be used as a KPI.*

Question 5
Which of the following metrics is useful in assisting you to determine the effectiveness of the Change Management process?
A. an increase in the number of recorded Request for Changes (RFCs) per period
B. an increase in the number of rejected Request for Changes (RFCs)
C. an increase in the number of Request for Changes (RFCs) being built

A. *Incorrect. This number shows the productivity of the Change Management process.*
B. **Correct.** *To measure the effectiveness of the Change process it is advisable to look at the workload at various key points throughout the process. An increase in the number of rejected RFCs indicates that the instructions to submit RFC are not being followed, are misunderstood, are too complicated or the rules to accept a change are too rigid. This indicates that the communication has failed and that the education and training is lacking.*
C. *Incorrect. This number shows the productivity of the Change Management process.*

Question 6
A system development project was recently started. The Project Manager has asked the Release Manager to demonstrate the effectiveness of this process during the implementation stage.

Which Key Performance Indicator (KPI) will be used in the report?
A. accurate distribution of Releases
B. secure and accurate management of the Definitive Software Library (DSL)
C. the planned composition of Releases matching the actual composition

A. **Correct.** *In this case Release Management assists Project Management in implementing a Release but does not take control.*
     Ref. 9.7.1, 9.8.5 of Service Support (OGC)
B. *Incorrect. This KPI monitors effectiveness of activities under control of Release Management.*
C. *Incorrect. This KPI monitors effectiveness of activities under control of Release Management.*

Question 7

At organization "X" the various business managers usually communicate directly with the developers and programmers when they require new functionalities. You have been tasked to communicate to the business about following the Release and Control processes, and to submit their requests to the Change Management process.

Which of the following best reflects the tone of your communication to the business managers?
A. You have to be firm and enforce the process. Business managers must submit their Change Requests to the change process. There will be severe repercussions for not following the process.
B. You need to create a communication plan outlining the benefits of the Release and Control processes so that resources can be properly planned and Changes documented, assessed and implemented.
C. You need to explain the various categories of Changes to the business managers and allow them to submit standard pre-approved Changes directly to the developers/programmers as most requests for functionalities are minor in nature.

A. *Incorrect. You need their cooperation in this transition.*
B. ***Correct.*** *You need to sell the benefits of the process.*
C. *Incorrect. You need to implement the process consistently.*

Question 8

Financial Management for IT Services wants to reduce the Total Cost of Ownership for client machines in the organization.

Which information does Financial Management for IT Services need from Configuration Management?
A. Asset Management information regarding the desktop PCs, laptops and software
B. Configuration Management information regarding all hardware
C. Configuration Management information regarding all hardware and software

A. *Incorrect. This only informs about the purchase prices of hardware and software, but does not give information on costs for operating, support and maintenance.*
B. *Incorrect. This does not include the software information.*
C. ***Correct.*** *This gives information about the assets and the use of these assets (relationships) in an operational environment.*
   Ref. 7.6.2 of Service Support

Question 9

License management is part of the Release and Control processes.

Which process has to verify the software with the accompanying licenses?
A. Change Management
B. Configuration Management
C. Release Management

A.   *Incorrect. License management is not an activiy of Change Management.*
B.   **Correct.** *Configuration Management should verify that secure master copies of software, documentation, data, licenses and agreements for supply, warranty and maintenance are lodged within the Configuration Management Database (CMDB) or Definitive Software Library (DSL).*
     Ref. 7.6.3 of Service Support (OGC)
C.   *Incorrect. License management is not an activiy of Release Management.*

Question 10

Each Configuration Item (CI) must be given a unique identification code. This code identifies the CI in the Configuration Management Database (CMDB) and is also the code that is physically affixed to the CI by means of a label. You decide to use the following coding for the PCs: WS-UT1-XXX, where UT1 stands for the Utrecht branch, 1st floor, and XXX is a three-digit serial number.

Is this a correct naming convention?
A.   No, this code contains too much unnecessary and dynamic information, which can all be found in the CMDB.
B.   Yes, by including the branch and floor in the code, in the case of failure it can be seen straight away where the problem is located.
C.   Yes, in view of the limited growth of the branches, a three-digit serial number is more than adequate.

A.   **Correct.** *An identification code must contain as little implicit information as possible. This code is full of it (type, branch, floor). The best thing is to simply give a serial number (e.g. a barcode). All the relevant information can be looked up in the CMDB. It is not likely that the CI type will change (e.g. WSXXXX) and such a code is therefore acceptable.*
     Ref. 7.6.2 of Service Support (OGC)
B.   *Incorrect. Information that can change quickly, like the location of the CI, is not allowed.*
C.   *Incorrect. It is not certain that the growth stays limited.*

Question 11

You want to be able to display the entire life cycle of a Configuration Item (CI), from order to deletion, by giving it a status.

Which is a correct way to do this?
A.   ORDERED, STOCK, TEST, LIVE, REPAIR, ARCHIVED, DELETED
B.   ORDERED, STOCK, TEST, PRODUCTION, OUT OF ORDER, ARCHIVED, DELETED
C.   Request for Change (RFC), STOCK, TEST, LIVE, OUT OF ORDER, ARCHIVED, DELETED

A.   **Correct.** *With the statuses mentioned, the life cycle of a CI can be followed perfectly well. For software developed in-house, sometimes the statuses BUILD, TEST and/or ACCEPTANCE are added. You could consider whether such phases of a project are desirable as a status.*
     Ref. 7.6.4 of Service Support (OGC)

B. *Incorrect. Production is not part of the life cycle within the service organization.*
C. *Incorrect. RFC is not part of the life cycle of a CI.*

Question 12
What serves as input for the design, build and configuration of a Release?
A. accepted Releases after successful testing
B. Release assembly instructions
C. Release definition and Release plans

A. *Incorrect. Testing and acceptance take place after designing, building and configuring a Release.*
B . *Incorrect. These are output products of design, build and configuration.*
C. **Correct.** *Release definition and Release plans serve as input for the design, build and configuration of a Release.*
    Ref. 9.6.2 of Service Support

Question 13
New software is implemented in a distributed environment. One of the objectives is to ensure the option of fast back-out from Changes across the network.

What needs to be in place to ensure this fast back-out?
A. limited software installation on workstations
B. the possibility to freeze failing applications
C. single user sign-on to all systems

A. *Incorrect. Workstations should have access to all systems but the purpose is not to ensure a fast back-out.*
B. **Correct.** *When freezing failing applications, distribution and implementation can be interrupted and the original situation can be restored as soon as possible.*
    Ref. Annex 9B of Service Support (OGC)
C. *Incorrect. Users should have a single sign-on but the purpose is not to ensure a fast back-out.*

Question 14
The Configuration Management Database (CMDB) is updated and referred to throughout the Release Management process.

Should the definition of planned Releases be recorded in the CMDB?
A. No, because the definition of planned Releases is not a Configuration Item (CI).
B. No, because the definition of planned Releases is not yet an update of the information in the CMDB.
C. Yes, because the definition of planned Releases is the basis for the design, build and configuration of the Release.

A. *Incorrect. The definition of planned Releases should be recorded in the CMDB (see C).*
B. *Incorrect. The definition is not an update but it will affect CIs.*
C. **Correct.** *The definition of planned Releases is input for the design, build and configure and it is therefore part of the documentation of the Release.*
    Ref. 9.3.8 of Service Support (OGC)

Question 15

What does the Definitive Hardware Store (DHS) contain?

A. hardware spare parts for maintaining the systems
B. hardware spares to be used for additional systems or for the recovery of major Incidents
C. information about hardware to roll-out as part of a Release

A.   Incorrect. In the DHS there are no parts, there are assemblies.
*B.   **Correct.** Hardware spares are spare components and assemblies that are maintained at the same level as the comparative systems within the live environment.*
     Ref. 9.3.7 of Service Support (OGC)
C.   Incorrect. Information about hardware is kept in the Configuration Management Database (CMDB).

Question 16

The general IT Manager has noticed that staff are spending a lot of time reviewing Changes.

What is a purpose of Change reviews?

A. to establish that all Changes have been assessed and prioritized
B. to establish that the Change was implemented on time and within the specified cost limitations
C. to establish that the Forward Schedule of Changes (FSC) has been produced and distributed on time

A.   Incorrect. This is done before the implementation of the Change.
*B.   **Correct.** The purpose of a review is to see that the Change was implemented on time and to cost.*
     Ref. 8.5.12 of Service Support (OGC)
C.   Incorrect. This is done before the implementation of the Change.

Question 17

What is an activity when reviewing a roll-out plan?

A. check if the roll-out plan requires any adjustment of the organizations release policy
B. check if the roll-out plan fits in with established Service Management and Support procedures
C. check if the roll-out plan has been authorized by the Change requester

A.   Incorrect.
*B.   **Correct.** In A, the organization's release policy determines the roll-out planning possibilities, not the other way around. Option C. The Change requester is involved in the Change Advisory Board (CAB) meeting when assessing the Request for Change (RFC), in testing the change and in acceptance of the implemented change. Authorization for implementing the release to the live environment is granted in the CAB meeting when scheduling changes.*
     Ref. Annex 9A, 9.6.3, 9.6.4 of Service Support (OGC)
C.   Incorrect.

Question 18
The Change Management staff is swamped with mail messages from Change builders, testers and other staff reporting the status or progress of specific Changes.

How can this be prevented?
A. ask Change builders, testers and other staff to hold back until the Change is ready for implementation
B. allocate more Change Management staff
C. authorize Change builders, testers and other staff to add information to Change records

A. *Incorrect. The updates must be recorded.*
B. *Incorrect. This is expensive and unnecessary.*
C. **Correct.** *The tool should enable Change Management staff, change builders, testers and other staff to add information to Change records.*
Ref. 8.8 of Service Support (OGC)

Question 19
A car manufacturer has a number of branches worldwide. The management wants to use Voice Over IP to reduce costs. The IT Service Organization is asked to provide this new service.

What are the consequences for the Change, Release and Configuration Management procedures?
A. adjustment of the Change Management plan
B. an extension of the Configuration Management Database (CMDB)
C. none, just another service to manage

A. **Correct.** *The Release policy (as part of the Change Management plan) has to be extended when an organization adopts a new technical infrastructure. New procedures for Release Management are expected.*
Ref. 8.1 of Service Support (OGC).
B. *Incorrect. This is not a procedure but the execution of a procedure.*
C. *Incorrect. A new service will affect existing procedures.*

Question 20
The Service Manager has issued an audit of the Change Management process for compliance with all Service Support processes next month.

Which item should be included in the examination?
A. Change Advisory Board (CAB) minutes
B. Change model
C. Request for Change (RFC) form

A. **Correct.** *The audit should include an examination of the following items: randomly selected RFCs, change records, CAB minutes, Forward Schedule of Changes (FSC) and records of implemented Changes.*
Ref. 8.7.1 of Service Support (OGC)

B. *Incorrect. This can be audited by Change Management internally.*
C. *Incorrect. This can be audited by Change Management internally.*

Annex E Links & Literature

E1. Literature

Subject	Title	Publisher	ISBN
Service Management	Service Support	OGC / TSO	0113300158
Service Management	Service Delivery	OGC / TSO	0113300174
Service Management	Security Management	OGC / TSO	011330014X
Service Management	Introduction to ITIL	itSMF/TSO	0113309732
Service Management	Small-Scale Implementation	OGC/TSO	0113309805
Applications	Application Management	OGC / TSO	0113308663
Applications	Software Asset Management	OGC / TSO	0113309430
Infrastructure	ICT Infrastructure Management	OGC / TSO	0113308655
Business	Business Perspective Vol 1	OGC / TSO	0113308949
Business	Business Perspective Vol 2	OGC / TSO	0113309694
Implementation	Planning to Implement Service Management	OGC / TSO	0113308779

E2. Relevant web sites

OGC	http://www.ogc.gov.uk
ITIL	http://www.itil.co.uk
EXIN	http://www.exin-exams.com
ISEB	http://www.bcs.org.uk/iseb
itSMF International	http://www.itsmf.org
ITSM PORTAL	http://en.itsmportal.net/
Loyalist College	http://www.itilexams.com
TÜV SÜD Akademie	http://www.bildung4me.de/
ISO20000	http://www.isoiec20000certification.com/

Index of templates and samples

Roles & responsibilities

Samples & tips

Templates

Index